Dedication

To my parents, who launched my lifelong love affair with wild places, and to my children, for whom I hope to do the same.

Includes 1996 UPDATE

See page 177, following index.

50
BEST
SHORT HIKES
in
Yosemite and Sequoia/Kings Canyon

John Krist

WILDERNESS PRESS
BERKELEY

Acknowledgments

I'd like to thank Malinee Crapsey and the interpretive staff at Sequoia and Kings Canyon National Parks for reviewing portions of the manuscript for accuracy. Errors that remain are my fault, not theirs. And most of all I want to thank my wife, Jean, who gave up two years' worth of vacations and perhaps a bit of sanity so I could hit the trails. This book is as much hers as it is mine.

FIRST EDITION June 1993
Second printing July 1994
Third printing July 1996

Copyright © 1993 by John Krist
Photos and maps by the author except as noted
Design by Thomas Winnett and Kathy Morey
Cover design by Larry B. Van Dyke
Cover photo © 1993 by Ed Cooper

Library of Congress Card Number 93-17151
ISBN 0-89997-132-2

Manufactured in the United States of America
Published by Wilderness Press
      2440 Bancroft Way
      Berkeley, CA 94704
      (510) 843-8080
      FAX (510) 548-1355

      Write, call or fax for free catalog

Library of Congress Cataloging-in-Publication Data

Krist, John, 1958-
    50 best short hikes in Yosemite and Sequoia/Kings Canyon / John Krist
      p. cm.
    Includes bibliographical references (p.) and index.
    ISBN 0-89997-132-6
    1. Hiking—California—Yosemite National Park—Guidebooks.
    2. Hiking—California—Sequoia National Park—Guidebooks.
    3. Hiking—California—Kings Canyon National Park—Guidebooks.
    4. Yosemite National Park (Calif.)—Guidebooks. 5. Sequoia National
Park (Calif.)—Guidebooks. 6. Kings Canyon National Park (Calif.)—
Guidebooks.   I. Title.   II. Title: Fifty best short hikes in
Yosemite and Sequoia/Kings Canyon.
GV199.42.C22Y6745 1993
796.5'1'097944—dc20   93-17151
                                  CIP

Table of Contents

Highway Access

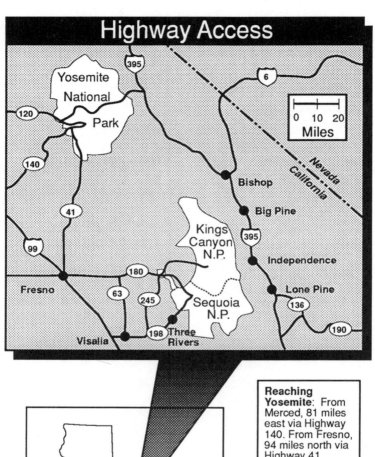

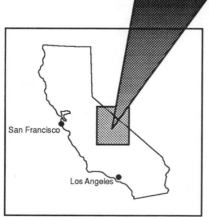

Reaching Yosemite: From Merced, 81 miles east via Highway 140. From Fresno, 94 miles north via Highway 41.

Reaching Sequoia: From Visalia, 35 miles east via Highway 198.

Reaching Kings Canyon: From Fresno, 55 miles east via Highway 180.

Introduction

Using this Book

Together, Yosemite, Sequoia and Kings Canyon national parks encompass more than 2,500 square miles of the Sierra Nevada range. Within them lie countless miles of trails, leading through some of the most spectacular scenery in North America. From paved, level pathways suitable for wheelchair travel to precipitous routes blasted out of sheer cliff faces, they offer an inexhaustible variety of experiences for those who would escape the cocoon of the family car and see the country as it should be seen.

With so many trails to choose from, the greatest challenge to the self-propelled traveler isn't finding a route into the high country, it's deciding which of the many alternatives to pick.

If you have unlimited time and few responsibilities, even this is not a problem. You can simply unfold a map and pick any route that stirs your imagination. But if you're a parent—or just busy, like so many adults in these days of two-career households—things are a bit more complicated. Your time is limited. And if your traveling companions are children, your mobility is likewise constrained.

But this doesn't mean you no longer feel the need to trade city streets and the urban scent of auto exhaust for soul-clearing mountain vistas and the perfume of pine. If anything, you need more than ever to feel the bones of the earth beneath your feet, to savor the music of falling water and the song of wind in the forest canopy. There is no greater antidote to the stress of modern urban life or the manifold strains of parenthood

If you have children—or just don't have the time for the long, strenuous hikes described by most trail guides—then this book was written with you in mind. The hikes it describes have been selected because they offer a maximum return for a moderate investment in time and effort. They range from easy nature trails that can be walked in an hour even by young children, to slightly more challenging routes suitable for a long day hike or a leisurely overnight backpacking trip.

The bulk of this book is divided into two sections, one for Yosemite and the other for Sequoia and Kings Canyon, since the latter two are contiguous and administered as a single unit. Within each section, the hikes are grouped according to where they originate, generally near a major visitor center or campground. Precise directions to the trailheads are provided, as well as information about camping, permits and reservations, and the availability of water, parking and restrooms.

Each section opens with an overview of the park's human and geological history, as well as the flora and fauna you're likely to encounter, in the hope that such information will make your hikes more satisfying. It is not within the scope of this book, however, to present an extensive or detailed guide to any of those subjects. For readers interested in exploring the subjects in greater depth, some recommended reading is provided. Visitors to the parks may also learn more by participating in the many guided walks and educational activities conducted during the summer by rangers.

Each trail description is preceded by a summary listing the mileage from start to finish, level of difficulty, starting elevation, highest or lowest point on the trail, and United States Geological Survey topographic map or maps covering the area. No hike in this guide exceeds 10 miles, which in the author's experience is the limit for a pleasant, casually paced day afoot.

As a special aid to hikers with children, each trail has been assigned a "child rating" that gives the minimum age at which a youngster might reasonably be expected to complete the hike under his or her own power. In general, easy nature trails of a mile or less are considered suitable for kids three and up, while those of 1 to 5 miles that do not involve strenuous climbs are rated for youngsters five and older. For the purposes of this book, hikes of more than 5 miles, and shorter trips that include steep ascents, are considered suitable only for children 10 and older.

Keep in mind, however, that children vary greatly in stamina, determination and distractibility, and a hike that would prove easy for one five-year-old might as well be an ascent of Mt. Whitney for another child of the same age. View the guide as only a rough estimation, prepare to move slowly, and be ready to turn back at any time even if you haven't reached your objective—unless you don't mind hiking back to your car or campsite with a cranky or sleeping child on your shoulders.

As you'll quickly discover, hiking with children is most rewarding when your goal is not to see how much terrain you can cover in one day, but to see each tree, granite boulder and fallen pine cone through their eyes.

Trail Etiquette

Because of their proximity to the major metropolitan areas in the nation's most populous state, Yosemite, Kings Canyon and Sequoia national parks are quite busy in the summertime. Although only a small fraction of the millions who enter the parks each year venture away from the roads and developed campgrounds, trail use is heavy enough to force the Park Service to regulate access to the backcountry for overnight visitors.

Although the very notion of a quota system for those who are trying to leave the crowds and noise of civilization behind is ironic and disheartening, the need for such regulation can't be denied. Overuse is a very real problem on the most popular Sierra trails; one look at the knee-deep ruts that mar Tuolumne Meadows along the popular Pacific Crest Trail leaves no doubt of the damage that can be inflicted on such a lovely and fragile spot simply by the impact of thousands of booted feet.

Because of their accessibility and proximity to visitor centers, many of the trails in this book are heavily traveled. To keep damage to a minimum—and to lessen the burden on park workers handicapped by inadequate maintenance budgets—please observe a few elementary rules when hiking.

1. Stay on the trail. Shortcuts hasten erosion, destroy vegetation, multiply the number of unsightly footpaths and can get you into trouble. The Park Service has enough to do without rescuing stranded travelers or treating injuries produced when rocks dislodged by amateur trailblazers land on the heads of unsuspecting fellow hikers.

2. Pack out your trash. It shouldn't be necessary to remind anyone of this. Still, every backcountry traveler has come across soft-drink cans, film containers, candy wrappers or worse on the trail, and each year volunteers haul tons of garbage from popular lakes and other destinations. If you can carry it in, you can certainly carry it out. Some hikers, in fact, make it a point to carry out more than they carried in.

3. Keep the water pure. Do not bathe or wash your dishes in rivers or lakes; even so-called biodegradable soap is harmful to the aquatic ecosystem. Park regulations stipulate that you camp at least 100 feet from water, which means avoiding some attractive back-country camp sites established through repeated use before the restriction was adopted. Likewise, dispose of human waste at least that far away from the water—farther if possible—in a hole at least 6 inches deep. Some trail guides recommend burning the used toilet paper, because animals so often dig up and scatter it, but that poses a fire hazard if not done carefully. You should never leave anything smoldering, whether it's your campfire or your latrine. Be aware that the high organic content of the humus covering the forest floor makes it flammable. The safest and soundest way to minimize the impact of your presence is to carry the toilet paper back out in a sealed plastic bag. Granted, many will find this option somewhat revolting, but so is the sight of used toilet paper in the backcountry.

4. Be polite. Many hikers despise the presence of pack animals in the wilderness, and there's no denying that horses and mules pulverize the trails, foul water supplies, damage vegetation and leave smelly droppings that attract flies. Still, current regulations allow them on the trails, and they must be given the right-of-way when encountered by hikers. Be likewise respectful toward your fellow foot-travelers: Let faster-moving parties pass, keep noise to a minimum, acknowledge the desire for solitude that sends many into the mountains in the first place. Obey park rules, which prohibit pets, vehicles (including bicycles) and firearms on the trails.

Hiking Safety

Every year people die or are seriously hurt in the mountains, and although most such incidents can be blamed on recklessness or ignorance, they serve as a reminder that the Sierra is still a wild place indifferent to the well-being of human visitors. Even if you plan to spend no more than a few hours on the trail, you should observe a few elementary, common-sense precautions.

1. Tell someone where you're going. Depending on how far ahead you like to plan, this can be someone at home, or you can leave a note in your car. But don't tape that note to the windshield unless you want to learn firsthand of another problem that occasionally crops up in the busy national parks: crime.

2. Beware of untreated water. There's something uniquely satisfying about dipping your drink straight from a singing mountain stream, but there is a good chance that the crystalline water is contaminated with a protozoan called *Giardia lamblia*, which loves to establish residence in the human intestinal tract. Authorities disagree on the actual likelihood of infection for the hiker who takes only an occasional drink from a contaminated stream, but anyone who has suffered the violent cramps, diarrhea, bloating and exhaustion of giardiasis will tell you it is not worth risking. Fill your water bottle from a safe source before you set out. If your trip will last overnight, boil, filter or chemically treat water you obtain from surface sources.

3. Be careful near rivers. Sierra water is cold, and even a deceptively small stream may be moving with enough force to sweep you off your feet. Once you're in, the cold will shock and disorient you, as the current does its best to slam you headfirst into rocks. And it should go without saying that wading or swimming above a waterfall is a bad idea, but deaths have been recorded in Yosemite where, despite abundant and strident warning signs, people have lost their footing and been swept over the magnificent cataracts that decorate the walls of the valley. Drowning is also the leading cause of death in Sequoia-Kings Canyon.

4. Stay away from wildlife. Park rules are specific and strict when it comes to storing food and dealing with black bears, which can be a considerable nuisance virtually everywhere in the parks. Read and follow the regulations, which are posted in campgrounds and handed out with backcountry permits. Squirrels and chipmunks can carry rabies and fleas that transmit bubonic plague, and should not be fed or handled. Mosquitos are perhaps the most annoying form of Sierran wildlife, and in early season can make you quite miserable. Bring a good insect repellent. The most effective are those containing N,N-diethyl-meta-toluamide, more commonly known as DEET. Rattlesnakes are present but seldom pose a threat as long as you leave them alone and avoid sticking your hands or feet suddenly into places you can't see. Ticks may also be found in foothill areas, and some carry Lyme disease. Read and heed the warnings posted at trailheads and ranger stations.

5. Prepare for the weather. Even in summer, conditions can change rapidly in the mountains, and that stylish hiking ensemble of shorts and T-shirt that seemed perfectly adequate at noon may seem pitifully scant four hours later when the wind picks up and an afternoon thunderstorm blows in. Hypothermia—the rapid, uncontrolled loss of your body heat—can set in even if the temperature is nowhere near freezing, and it can kill you. Always carry something warm and have the sense to turn back if conditions arise that you are not prepared for. Likewise, protect yourself against the sun. Trails with a southern exposure can be quite hot in the afternoon, and the chance of sunburn is greater at high altitudes, where the thinner atmosphere blocks fewer of the sun's ultraviolet rays.

6. Know where you're going. The trails described in this book are all well-marked and require no special bushwhacking skills to follow. Still, you'll get more out of your hike if you study your route beforehand, carry this guide with you and bring the appropriate topographic map, which is listed in each trail description. The map and a compass—plus the ability to use them—will help you identify landmarks visible as you travel, which adds greatly to the enjoyment of a hike. They'll also help keep you from getting lost, something that detracts greatly from the enjoyment of a hike.

7. Don't overdo it. Remember that your body will take some time to adapt to the scarcity of oxygen in the air at high altitudes. Unless you give yourself a day or two to acclimate, you are likely to find yourself suffering some symptoms of altitude sickness—headache, nausea, fatigue—if you push yourself too far or climb too high too soon. Relax and take it easy. The hikes in this book are geared toward the average hiker in decent physical condition, not triathletes or marathon-runners. Set a comfortable pace and you'll get where you're going without any problem.

8. Equip yourself properly. Carry water and a first-aid kit even on short hikes. Wear appropriate footgear. Sturdy sneakers may be fine on level meadow trails, but you'll need something offering more ankle support and protection if you'll be carrying a child on your back, or traveling a rocky or steep route. Pack snacks for quick energy. And bring this guide.

Hiking With Kids

Hiking poses special challenges when children are among your companions. Some of those challenges are physical, others are psychological. In both cases, it pays to be prepared.

In general, a baby is old enough for hiking when it can hold up its head without difficulty, something most infants are capable of by the age of six months. In some ways, this is the best age at which to bring children on the trail, mainly because they'll sleep much of the time, they don't weigh much and they'll stay where you put them when you stop for a lunch break or an hour of wool-gathering on the shore of a mountain lake. On the other hand, an infant isn't very good at conversation, is decidedly unawed by cascading waterfalls, close encounters with mule deer or the ruddy magnificence of a giant sequoia, and probably won't even notice the spectacular view from a rocky pinnacle. Each age brings with it a unique combination of advantages and disadvantages.

There are several lightweight child-carriers on the market which will allow you to carry an infant in relative comfort even on a long day hike. Their thin shoulder pads and belts are not adequate, however, once the child reaches about 20 pounds. For toddlers you'll need a heavier pack, one designed—like any good standard

Thomas Winnett

In a Forest Service campground

backpack—to transfer most of the weight to your hips. Several models of these heavier child-carriers are available, although they are costly. Shop carefully, or inquire about rentals. Look for strong construction, plenty of adjustability to ensure your child won't outgrow it quickly, ample padding in the shoulder straps and hip belt, and storage for the many items you'll need to carry. Take time in the store to try it out with a real kid on board. Both of you need to be happy with the pack if you hope to enjoy your hikes.

Children develop at different rates, so it is risky to generalize. But you can probably count on carrying your youngster on most hikes until the age of three. After that, you'll need the pack for trails longer than a couple of miles, or those that involve much climbing. From five on, with judicious trip selection, your child should be able to make it most of the way on his or her own.

Even if you are an experienced backpacker, carrying a child on your back will pose new challenges. For one thing, 30 pounds of kid does not behave like 30 pounds of tent, stove, sleeping bag, cookset and clothing. Kids move, throwing you off balance at critical moments—halfway across a log bridge, for example. As cargo, a seated child has a lower center of gravity than a well-packed load of inanimate objects, making it almost impossible to achieve ideal weight distribution. Practice by carrying the child around town before venturing into the unpredictable backcountry.

There are a few other things to keep in mind when preparing to take your infant or toddler on the trail.

1. Pack snacks such as bite-size pieces of fruit, raisins and crackers in small plastic bags so your child can munch as you walk. This will help prevent fussiness in a child riding in a pack, and will give an energy boost to one on foot.

2. Bring spare diapers and a sealable plastic bag in which to store them when they're soiled. Do not bury disposables or wash cloth diapers in streams or lakes.

3. Remember to stop every hour or so and remove your child from the pack. A toddler will need to run around a bit, and an infant will welcome the change in position.

4. Apply sunscreen to your child, keeping in mind that sunburn occurs much more quickly at high altitudes.

5. If the weather is cold, keep your child bundled up. You might not be cold, but you're hauling a pack full of kid up the mountain. A child kept motionless in a backpack will become chilled long before you do.

6. If the weather is hot, a T-shirt and diaper are probably all you'll need to dress your child in. Hemmed in by the unbreathable nylon of most pack bodies, your youngster may have trouble staying cool. A hat is a good idea, although it's a rare child who won't send it sailing into the underbrush. Clamping a small umbrella to the pack frame to provide shade is a good idea, too, but only if you will be traversing open country. In dense forest or brush it will only be a nuisance as it catches on overhanging branches.

7. Remember insect repellent, especially in early summer when mosquitos are most numerous. On an older child it is safe to use any good commercial repellent, but they can be toxic for very small infants. For babies you'll need to try one of the less effective but safer organic alternatives. Some people swear by a product that was not developed as a bug repellent but as a bath oil, Avon's Skin-So-Soft, which is harmless and appears to have some effect in warding off biting bugs. Also recommended for infants are repellents containing the pesticide permethrin, which should be applied to clothing, not skin, and is much less toxic than DEET. When in doubt, consult your pediatrician.

8. Scale back your expectations. Whether your child is riding on your back or tramping at your side, he or she will determine the pace. Some youngsters will plug along at a good clip or ride uncomplainingly for hours in a backpack, while others stop to examine in minute detail every stick, rock, pine cone and bird feather they come across. Remember that young children are not goal-oriented, and cannot be urged along by promising a beautiful view around the next corner. Neither of you will enjoy the trip if you spend most of your time urging your child to move faster or to sit sill in the pack and keep quiet. Resign yourself to a slower pace than you are used to, and enjoy the natural inquisitiveness that children display whenever they encounter unfamiliar sights and sounds—even if it takes the form of unanswerable questions repeated insistently during a steep ascent that has robbed you of breath.

A Note About Maps

For the day hikes described in this book, topographic maps are recommended but not essential. All the trails are well-used and easy to follow, and the trip descriptions themselves should keep you from taking a wrong turn anywhere along the way. In addition, this book itself contains maps that will guide you to the trailheads and give you a general idea of the surrounding features. Still, carrying a topo map—and knowing how to use it—will add to your peace of mind and help you learn more about the countryside you're exploring.

Each trip description identifies the relevant 15' and 7.5' topographic quadrangles produced by the United States Geological Survey, which provide details about terrain that the maps published in this book omit in the interest of clarity. There's a reason for listing two types of USGS maps.

The 15' maps cover an area 15 minutes of latitude by 15 minutes of longitude, or roughly 245 square miles in the area of this book. For many years they were the standard upon which backcountry travelers relied to identify natural and man-made features of the countryside, and to anticipate the ups and downs of the trail. With their scale of 1 mile to the inch, the 15' series provided adequate detail and still covered a large area, so it was seldom necessary to carry more than one or two maps on any but the longest trips.

The Geological Survey, however, has discontinued publication of most of the 15' maps. Instead, the government is updating the map data and switching to a series of 7.5' quadrangles, which have a scale of 0.38 mile to the inch.

The added detail in the 7.5' maps is nice, but it means hikers now will have to buy—and carry—four maps to cover an area that used to be depicted on one. This means added expense and inconvenience.

It may still be possible to purchase some of the 15' maps at the outlets where they've always been available, such as good sporting-goods and backpacking-equipment stores, so this book identifies the one you'll need for each hike. Park visitor centers also stock many of them, but the stock is dwindling. That's why the book also identifies the 7.5' map—or maps—for each hike.

A word of caution: Some new maps bear the same names as an old 15' quadrangle, but of course don't cover the same territory. Make sure you know which map you are buying. The series is identified on the map itself, in the upper or lower right-hand corner.

If your local sporting goods store doesn't have what you need, USGS topographic maps may be ordered from the survey itself at:

U.S. Geological Survey
Box 25286, Federal Center
Denver, CO 80225

They may also be purchased in person during business hours at these survey offices:

7638 Federal Building
300 N. Los Angeles St.
Los Angeles, CA

345 Middlefield Road
Menlo Park, CA

The 15' series of topo maps is being kept from complete extinction by Wilderness Press, which publishes its own versions of many of the most popular Sierra quadrangles and plans to expand its list of offerings to fill some of the void being left by the Geological Survey. These maps feature more accurate trail markings than the USGS versions, and may be either ordered from or purchased in person at the following addresses:

The Map Center
2440 Bancroft Way
Berkeley, CA 94704
Phone: (510) 841-MAPS

The Map Center
63 Washington St.
Santa Clara, CA 95050
Phone: (408) 296-MAPS

The Map Centers also stock all the 7.5' maps for California.   ■

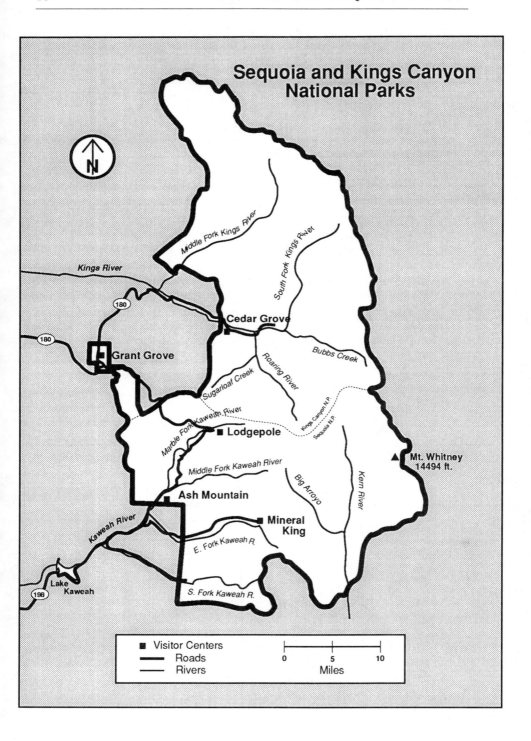

Sequoia and Kings Canyon
National Parks

Sequoia and Kings Canyon

Geological History

Rock defines the country you are in, by the way its surfaces reflect light, by the way it erodes under the attack of ice, rain and running water, and even by the type of soil it forms when it decomposes. The glacier-polished granite of the high country shines likes a mirror in direct sunlight, and glows with soft luminosity under a summer moon. The black, brown and rust colors of volcanic landscapes seem to absorb sunlight, creating a landscape of somber mood. Flowers may reflect the chemical content of minerals in the soil by the color of their blooms; streams bob and weave according to the resistance of the stone in their path.

You don't have to know the difference between feldspar and pyroxene to enjoy a hike in the Sierra Nevada. But a basic understanding of the forces that shaped the terrain—as well as a passing familiarity with the rock types that are the building blocks of the scenery around you—will help you derive more from your visit.

Sequoia and Kings Canyon national parks are in the southern part of the Sierra Nevada, the largest single mountain range in the United States. It stretches nearly 400 miles, from Tehachapi Pass in the south to Lake Almanor in the north, and is 50 to 80 miles wide. It was given its name in 1776 by Spanish missionary Pedro Font, a member of the colonizing party that founded San Francisco, who looked eastward from the low, sunburned hills between San Francisco Bay and the Central Valley and reported that he espied "*una gran sierra nevada*," a great snowy range.

We can only guess at the vista that presented itself to Font. Today, thanks to urban growth, motor vehicles and modern agricultural practices, the crystalline air that 200 years ago allowed explorers to see snow-capped peaks from more than 120 miles away has been contaminated by dust and other particulates, and photochemical smog created largely by the state's millions of automobiles. Approaching from the west, it is seldom possible to see the mountains until you are virtually in them, and ozone is damaging trees in the range above the San Joaquin Valley.

But the range is still snowy, and it is indisputably great, nearly as large in area as the French, Swiss and Italian Alps combined. In structure, it is essentially a huge rectangular block, tilted slightly so that it presents a long, gentle incline on the west and a short, steep incline on the east. Kings Canyon and Sequoia National Parks contain two of its most noted features: Mt. Whitney, at 14,494 feet the highest peak in the Lower 48 states; and Kings Canyon, a gash in the earth that reaches 8200 feet in depth just outside the park, a spectacular chasm half again as deep as the Grand Canyon.

Geologists are uncertain about some of the specific events that formed the range, but there is a fair amount of agreement on the general outline of the story. It begins about 500 million years ago, when the region that is now the mountains was at the edge of the continent, lying beneath the sea. For hundreds of millions of years, sediment washing off the land was deposited in that sea, forming thick beds of shale and sandstone. During the same time, tiny aquatic creatures died by the trillions and added their shells to the mixture.

About 250 million years ago, the great, slowly moving plates of the earth's crust that form the North American continent and the Pacific Ocean floor begin colliding. The continent—with the yet-to-be-born Sierra at its leading edge—rode up over the oceanic plate, which dove below the continent and into the earth. There the diving rock melted from the heat and friction, and then it bubbled upward, pushing against the ancient sea sediments. In some cases the overlying rock was melted and incorporated into the molten *magma*; in other cases it was twisted, deformed and chemically altered by the heat below it, until none of the original sedimentary deposits retained their initial form.

The limestone formed by thick deposits of sea shells was transformed by the heat and pressure into marble, a remnant band of which is visible in Sequoia and Kings Canyon. Crystal and Boyden caves, popular visitor attractions, formed in this band of marble. The same pressures turned the other sediments into gneiss and schist, which may still be seen on Redwood Mountain and above the road to Giant Forest near Potwisha Campground.

This phase continued for more than 100 million years. Most of the magma cooled far below the surface, creating huge underground masses of stone called plutons. A series of these plutons form the granitic backbone of the Sierra we see today, and their formation was complete by about 80 million years ago.

The Sierra foundation had been laid at this point, but the mountains as we know them had yet to rise. First the low range created by the upwelling magma and the buckling pressure of tectonic collision was worn down to mere hills by erosion, which removed most of the metamorphosed sea sediments and exposed the granite.

Granite is a layman's term for the hard, salt-and-pepper stone that comprises early all the visible rock formations in Sequoia and Kings Canyon, as well as much of the rest of the Sierra Nevada. Geologists have refined the term and use a variety of labels for its different forms—granite, quartz monzonite, granodiorite—based on the relative proportions of different minerals in the mixture. It is composed primarily of glassy quartz, black flecks of mica and white or pinkish crystals of feldspar.

The process that gave the range the general shape we see today began only about 10 million years ago but is perhaps the least understood episode in the entire history of the Sierra Nevada. Although the precise mechanism is not known, the huge block of the range began to tilt rapidly. Most of the vertical movement took place on the east, producing the sheer face that towers nearly 2 miles above the Owens Valley.

The range is still rising, at times abruptly: On March 26, 1872, during a severe earthquake centered on the Alabama Hills Fault in the Owens Valley, the vertical difference between the summit of Mt. Whitney and the valley floor nearby increased by 12 feet. The quake, felt throughout California, destroyed the town of Lone Pine, where it killed 29 people—a tenth of the population.

About 3 million years ago, the final sculpting of the mountains began. As the climate cooled and annual snowfall began to exceed seasonal snowmelt, glaciers formed in alpine basins near the mountain summits and grew in size and strength. Slowly, inexorably they flowed downhill, carving, scraping and gouging away at the landscape, widening and deepening river valleys, plucking the faces from cliffs, rounding and polishing the granite bedrock of the mountains.

At the height of this ice age, glaciers as much as 4000 feet deep covered roughly 4000 square miles of the Sierra Nevada. The longest of these rivers of ice, the Tuolumne Glacier, stretched more than 60 miles, terminating in the Sierra foothills at an elevation of about 2000 feet. Evidence of their work abounds in Sequoia and Kings Canyon national parks, starting with Tokopah Valley, location of the popular Lodgepole visitor center and campground in Sequoia. The streamside camping area was buried by more than 500 feet of ice when the Tokopah Glacier occupied the valley,

Thomas Winnett

An erratic left by a glacier

polishing its granite walls and widening its profile from the V-shape of a river canyon to the telltale U-shape typical of ice-carved valleys. In Kings Canyon, the Cedar Grove campground and village lie on the banks of the South Fork Kings River, which flows in a valley smoothed and widened by a massive glacier.

The ice had mostly melted by about 10,000 years ago, but adventurous visitors to Kings Canyon National Park can find reminders of the great ice sheets in the shadow of summits along the Palisade Crest, in the remote northeast corner of the park, and the Glacier Divide, on the northern park boundary. These living glaciers are among about 70 that still dot the Sierra's high country, formed during a miniature ice age that began only a thousand years or so ago, during a period of lowered average worldwide temperatures. They serve as reminders of the great age of ice, which on the scale of geologic time ended only moments ago and might resume any time.

Human History

Information is scant regarding the earliest human occupation of the Sequoia-Kings Canyon area. Archaeological evidence indicates that people have lived in Central California, including parts of the Sierra Nevada, for at least 6,000 to 7,000 years, but relatively little investigation has been done within the parks themselves. Two significant sites have been excavated to some degree: Hospital Rock, a large village site where a picnic area now is located, near the Buckeye Flat Campground at the southern end of Sequoia; and in Kings Canyon near the Cedar Grove area.

But historical accounts of the indigenous population do exist, and coupled with the physical evidence uncovered by excavation they give us a fair idea of what sort of people were living in the park area at the time white explorers first arrived.

They were members of two distinct groups, speaking languages of widely different origins. In the high country and middle foothills lived the Monache, or Western Mono, whose language indicates they came originally from the east side of the mountains. Close relatives of the inhabitants of the Owens Valley, they spoke a Shoshonean language, giving them a common ancestry with Native Americans in the basin-and-range country of Nevada and Utah, and on the Colorado Plateau.

At the lower elevations, primarily in the Central Valley but extending into the lowest foothills, were the Yokuts, far more numerous and related by language to the loosely organized tribes that occupied the bulk of interior California. The Yokuts groups dominated the lower stretches of the Kaweah and Kings rivers, and probably had smaller populations in the foothills that were displaced starting about 500 or 600 years ago when the Monache crossed the Sierra crest and began establishing permanent populations on the western slopes.

By the time Europeans arrived, the Sequoia-Kings Canyon area was dominated by the Monache, who had divided into a number of distinct bands. Three of them occupied territory inside what would someday become the parks.

The Wobonuch group occupied the foothills west of Grant Grove, in the Kings River drainage. The Waksachi inhabited the upper foothill valleys near the headwaters of the North Fork of the Kaweah. In the summer, members of both groups moved into the higher country, establishing seasonal camps at what are now Dorst Campground, Grant Grove and Cedar Grove. A keen eye can still find evidence of those camps in the nearby bedrock mortars, holes carved into the granite by generations of women grinding acorns and other nuts.

Most of the Sequoia-Kings Canyon area was occupied by a third group, the Potwisha, who had large permanent villages at Hospital Rock and the campground that bears their name. Evidence of their summer camps has also been found at Giant Forest and Mineral King, as well as other higher-elevation sites.

In all, about 250 prehistoric camp or village sites have been identified in the two parks, indicating that Indians visited nearly every part of the region. Many of those same sites are popular stopping points for modern backpackers, who instinctively seek many of the same features as did their prehistoric predecessors when selecting a camping place: level ground, access to water, shade from the summer sun, shelter from the wind.

Acorns were a staple of the Monache diet, but they also hunted, fished and gathered other plant materials. Shelter was provided by small conical huts of cedar bark or thatch—replicas of which have been constructed near the Grant Grove Visitor Center—and for most of the year clothing was scant.

Although Spanish missionaries, soldiers and exploring parties established a strong presence on the California coast in the 18th century and made sporadic excursions into the Central Valley, for the most part they did not venture into the Sierra Nevada. One exploring party did pass near the base of the mountains in 1805, naming the San Joaquin and Kings rivers. The name of the latter is a contraction of the original Spanish label, *Rio de los Santos Reyes*, or River of the Holy Kings, indicating that the explorers camped there on January 6, the day of Epiphany, which marks the visit of the Magi to the infant Jesus.

An expedition the next year passed through the same area and went farther north, naming the Merced River and the area now occupied by the town of Mariposa, which drew its name from the swarms of butterflies *(mariposas)* found there.

The first white explorers didn't enter the Sequoia-Kings Canyon area until 1827, when trapper Jedediah Smith, seeking beaver, worked his way up the San Joaquin River and then tried to cross the Sierra by following the Kings River

Bedrock mortars at Hospital Rock Picnic Area

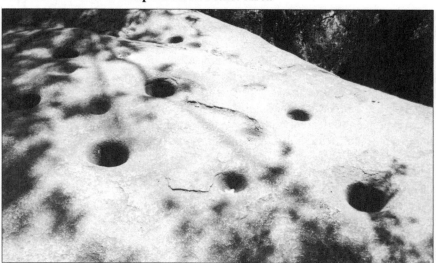

drainage. He failed because it was too early in the season and the snow was too deep. Moving north, he tried again and made the crossing—the first of the Sierra by a white man—near the Stanislaus River, north of Yosemite.

More trappers and explorers followed, including Lt. John Fremont of the U.S. Army Topographical Engineers, who made a rather ill-considered attempt to cross the Sierra in December 1844 by ascending the Kings River, whose deep canyon repeatedly misled explorers into thinking it offered an easy way through the mountains. Caught in the rugged high country by a winter storm, he and his party turned back, narrowly escaping to the valley floor with the loss of most of their livestock.

White settlers did not establish a permanent presence in the park region until after the start of the Gold Rush, which swelled the population of California and sent miners and ranchers into the mountains seeking either mineral riches or pasturage.

Hale Tharp, whose name can be found appended to a host of features in Sequoia National Park, was the first white to establish a more or less permanent residence in the park area. Originally drawn to California from his home in the Midwest to seek gold, he soon learned that there were better ways to make a living. In 1856 he selected the site for a cattle ranch on the lower Kaweah River, returning two years later to begin work on it. He traveled into the high country, becoming friendly with the native population at Hospital Rock and visiting Giant Forest. Soon he was using Log Meadow as a summer pasture for horses, living there in a fallen, fire-hollowed sequoia trunk he'd outfitted with a door and windows, while his cattle fattened on the rich grass of other mountain meadows.

He was followed by others, settlers who brought more cattle and sheep into the mountains, displacing the Monache bands from their home of centuries and introducing them to unfamiliar diseases such as smallpox, measles and scarlet fever. Cut off from their hunting and gathering grounds, and swept by epidemics, the Indians of the Sequoia-Kings Canyon area dwindled. By 1865, barely a decade after their first contact with white settlers, they were gone.

As the white population swelled, threats to the area's beauty and integrity as an ecosystem intensified. Having already eliminated the indigenous human population, settlers began destroying the native vegetation as well with their vast herds of grazing livestock. Miners came, too, although they were destined to be disappointed with the Sequoia-Kings Canyon area. Only in Mineral King Valley did mining gain a toehold, with the purported discovery in 1873 of silver ore. Shafts were sunk, stamp mills and smelters constructed, and many claims filed. Yet the small quantities of ore found in the valley proved impossible to turn into metal, and winter avalanches regularly destroyed the cabins, bunkhouses and other buildings associated with the mines. After absorbing the energy, fortunes and dreams of many hopeful miners, Mineral King returned nothing. By 1881 the mining boom, such as it was, had ended.

The most potentially damaging interest in the Sequoia-Kings Canyon area, however, came not from cattlemen, sheepherders or miners, but from loggers.

The giant sequoias were presumably known well by the indigenous people of the area. The first white man to see them is believed to have been Lt. Joseph Walker, who stumbled across a stand of sequoia near Yosemite Valley in 1833. Hale Tharp is generally credited with being the first white to see the groves in what is now Sequoia National Park, led there by a party of Potwishas in 1858.

Logging began in the Sequoia-Kings Canyon area nearly as soon as white settlers arrived. The richly forested western slopes of the southern Sierra provided ponderosa pine in abundance, and as early as 1856 a primitive sawmill was operating west of the Grant Grove area. By 1864 another mill was in operation near Grant Grove, on a site that today is flooded by Sequoia Lake, just outside the park boundary.

As logging technology improved and wagon roads extended farther into the mountains, the pace of logging increased. Flumes were built to carry logs into the valley below, and some of the most majestic stands of sequoia began to fall. Evidence of that activity can still be seen in Big Stump Basin, just inside the Kings Canyon Park entrance, and at Converse Basin, nearby in Sequoia National Forest, both of them cut over in the last two decades of the 1800s.

That more of the area's irreplaceable big trees weren't felled is probably due as much to their size and unsuitability for lumber as anything. The giants were difficult to handle once they'd been toppled, and the loggers sometimes used explosives to break the massive trunks into pieces small enough to work with. Too, the wood of the sequoia is brittle and tends to shatter. Most of a felled tree—50 to 75 percent—was wasted. The remainder was split into roofing shakes or fence posts.

As loggers felled the forests, and sheep and cattle grazed the mountain valleys bare, erosion in the high country increased, fouling streams and interfering with the flow of water to the irrigation-dependent farmers in the dry San Joaquin Valley. Alarmed by this potential threat, the valley residents, led by Visalia newspaper editor and publisher George Stewart, joined John Muir—who visited Kings Canyon in 1873 and 1875—and others in the embryonic conservation

Stump Meadow

movement to press for protection of the matchless scenic and natural resources of the Sequoia-Kings Canyon area.

Enlisting the support of elected officials, the preservation forces scored their first legislative victory in 1890. In September of that year, President Benjamin Harrison signed into law a bill withdrawing 76 square miles of forest land, centered around the South Fork Kaweah River, from sale to the public. As yet unnamed, it would be identified as Sequoia National Park a month later when the Department of the Interior issued regulations for its management.

Only six days after signing the act establishing Sequoia National Park, President Harrison signed a bill that established Yosemite National Park, tripled the acreage of Sequoia National Park and created yet another small reserve, later named General Grant National Park, which preserved the Grant Grove of sequoias.

In February 1893, Harrison signed a Presidential proclamation establishing the Sierra Forest Reserve, withdrawing from private ownership almost the entire southern Sierra Nevada from Yosemite to a point south of Sequoia National Park. Parts of that reserve would be incorporated into Sequoia National Park in July 1926, when the Kern Canyon and the Sierra crest around Mt. Whitney were added. In March 1940 other parts were designated as Kings Canyon National Park, which incorporated General Grant National Park and the wild and rugged country stretching north to Evolution Valley.

In June 1940 the Redwood Mountain area was added to Kings Canyon National Park, and in 1965 Cedar Grove and Tehipite Valley were incorporated, enlarging the park almost to its present size. The last piece of the patchwork was sewn into place in 1978, when Mineral King Valley was added, a victory for wilderness lovers who had battled plans by the Forest Service and Walt Disney Productions to turn the area into a ski resort complete with lifts, restaurants, hotels, chalets, snack bars and gas stations.

Standing today in the bowl of that valley, surrounded by steep, avalanche-scoured slopes and serenaded by the liquid music of the East Fork Kaweah River, it's hard to imagine what Mineral King would be like had the developers and the Forest Service had their way. And it's easy to see how this valley in some ways illustrates the difference between the Forest Service's guiding principle of "multiple use" and the Park Service's mission to preserve the landscape "unimpaired for future generations."

Plants and Animals

The vital statistics are impressive enough: It's the largest living thing on earth, weighing up to 2.7 million pounds. It grows more than 300 feet high, and its trunk can measure more than 100 feet in circumference. Resistant to fire, fungus and disease, it can live for more than 3,000 years.

But statistics do not do justice to the giant sequoia, the conifer John Muir called "the noblest of a noble race." To stand for the first time in a grove of the magnificent trees is to suffer a scrambling of the senses and a failure of descriptive power. The mind resists what the eyes are telling it, and speech seems inadequate to capture the experience.

The giant sequoia *(Sequoiadendron giganteum)* is related to the coast redwood *(Sequoia sempervirens)* and the more recently discovered dawn redwood *(Metasequoia glyptostrobides)*, all of which are descendants of a population that once grew as far north as the Bering Sea, and in Europe and Asia. That was before the last great ice age, however, which vastly reduced their range. Today the dawn redwood, smallest of the three, is found only in China, while the coast redwood, the tallest, grows naturally only in a narrow strip along the California coast from Monterey County to just north of the Oregon border. The giant sequoia is found only in scattered groves on the western slopes of the Sierra Nevada between Yosemite and Sequoia National Forest, just south of Sequoia National Park. It grows in groves only on moist, unglaciated ridges between 5,000 and 7,000 feet in elevation, where it is part of a conifer forest that includes white fir, sugar pine, yellow pines and incense-cedar.

The coast redwood is the tallest tree in the world, one specimen reaching 368 feet. But it is much slimmer in outline, and carries less bulk than the sequoia, also known as the big tree or Sierra redwood. What sets the sequoia apart from its cousins is the thickness of and lack of taper in its trunk, which give it far more mass. The largest specimen by volume is the General Sherman tree in Sequoia National Park: 275 feet tall, 103 feet in circumference at its base, 2,300–2,700 years old, and weighing 1,385 tons. Some of its branches are more than 7 feet in diameter.

Sequoia and Kings Canyon national parks preserve 30 of the 75 remaining groves of the big trees, Yosemite National Park also containing a few. One of the most magnificent stands, the one most likely to leave visitors speechless, is Giant Forest, heart of visitor activities in Sequoia National Park, a place that retains its ability to awe despite the proliferation of paved footpaths, parking lots, stores, cabins and other "improvements." At 1,800 acres, Giant Forest contains about 8,400 sequoias a foot or more in diameter, including four of the five largest trees in the world. More difficult to reach but pleasingly devoid of urban intrusions, the Redwood Mountain grove in Kings Canyon National Park covers about 3,100 acres and contains 15,800 trees of at least a foot in diameter. It is the largest sequoia grove in the world.

"Grove" is a somewhat misleading term when applied to the sequoia. Unlike the dense grouping most people envision when they hear the word, a sequoia grove consists of a loose collection of big trees intermingled with more numerically dominant species.

Giant sequoias grow only from seeds, contained in cones that seem absurdly small given the size of their parents. About the size of a hen's egg, the cones may hang on the branches for 20 years or more. A mature tree produces about 2,000 of them annually, together containing about half a million of the tiny oat-flake-sized seeds. Released in small quantities by feeding squirrels or beetles, or in thousands by the heat of fire, the seeds will sprout only if they fall on damp mineral soil that receives plenty of sunlight—characteristics found most commonly in areas that have been burned.

Recent study has confirmed the importance of periodic undergrowth-clearing brush fires in the propagation of the sequoia. After decades of total fire suppression, the official policy now in Sequoia and Kings Canyon national parks is to allow naturally occurring fires, those started by lightning, to burn in several specified management zones as long as strict conditions of moisture and weather are met. In addition, fires are set periodically in some areas of the parks to clear away the tons of tree limbs, brush and other organic material that accumulated during a century of strict fire suppression. By controlled burning of all that fuel, the potential for wildfires is reduced.

Death comes to a sequoia usually as a result of violence. Despite their incredible size the trees have a shallow root system, extending perhaps 100 feet from the trunk but no more than 3 to 5 feet deep. As a result, they are susceptible to toppling if undermined by erosion or weakened by root decay, especially when unbalanced by heavy snow or blasted by the ferocious winds that scour the Sierra during winter storms. Once down, however, they allow a flood of sunlight into the forest, often preparing the way for a new generation of offspring to germinate. The wood of a fallen giant, impregnated with tannin, resists insects and fungi, and may remain undecayed on the forest floor for hundreds of years.

The sequoia belt, although the primary attraction for many park visitors, is only one of several life zones found in Sequoia and Kings Canyon. These zones, which overlap, correspond roughly to different elevations, and are characterized by distinct plant and animal communities.

At the lowest elevations, such as those in the vicinity of Ash Mountain Park Headquarters at the southern entrance to Sequoia, is the foothill belt, characterized by oaks and chaparral—a hardy, drought-resistant grouping of shrubby plants including chamise, ceanothus and manzanita. Hot and dry in the summer, it extends generally from 1,250 to 5,000 feet in elevation.

Higher on the western slope, generally from 2,500 to 9,000 feet, is the mixed conifer belt, which outside the parks is the primary timber-producing region. Dominated by dense stands of enormous conifers such as Douglas fir, sugar pine, ponderosa pine and Jeffrey pine, as well as the more widely scattered sequoia and incense-cedar, the zone is dry and warm in summer, but in winter receives most of the mountains' precipitation. It is where most visitors to Sequoia and Kings Canyon spend their time, whether traveling on the Generals Highway or Kings Canyon Highway, or camping at Lodgepole, Grant Grove or Cedar Grove.

Higher still is the lodgepole pine-red fir belt, from 8,000 to 10,000 feet, the upper range of the dense conifer forest. During the winter this zone gets the heaviest snowfall, and here spring arrives late, sometimes not until late June. It is typified by the slopes above Mineral King Valley, as well as many remoter high-country valleys reachable only by foot.

Above this lies the subalpine belt, a sparsely forested region extending up to about 11,000 feet where only mountain hemlock, whitebark pine, foxtail pine and other hardy tree species grow. Higher still is the almost barren alpine zone, which extends above treeline and is home only to low-lying grasses, sedges and other creeping plants. Both zones are found on the mountain crests that separate the great drainage systems of the Sequoia-Kings Canyon area.

The boundaries between these zones are not distinct, and there is much overlap. Variations in average precipitation, temperature and exposure to sunlight due to topography create local microclimates where the species of several life zones intermingle.

Lovers of wildflowers will find plenty in the parks on which to feast their senses early in the season, especially in the meadows and along the banks of streams. The different types of flowering plants prefer different environments just as do the trees. At foothill elevations the grassy slopes are coated in springtime with a carpet of California poppy, lupine, creamy spires of yucca, monkeyflower, paintbrush, brodiaea, blazing star and baby blue eyes. At higher elevations the meadows are likely to be splashed by vivid sprays of gentian, shooting star, penstemon, paintbrush and mule ears.

Sequoia and Kings Canyon are also home to dozens of species of birds, from the common camp-robbing Steller's jay to the infrequently seen great horned owl. The Sequoia Natural History Association publishes a checklist.

Among the mammals most commonly seen by park visitors are the yellow-bellied marmot, which has been known to disable parked automobiles in Mineral King by gnawing on radiator hoses and electrical wiring, several species of squirrels and chipmunks, mule deer, and black bears, which actually vary in color from cinnamon to glossy jet.

Mountain hemlock

National Park Service

The relationship between bears and people in Sequoia and Kings Canyon has long been troublesome for park managers. In the 1920s visitors to Sequoia could congregate each evening at the park garbage dump in Giant Forest, where bleachers had been erected to give them a good view of bears pawing through the offal. Inevitably, however, there were confrontations between people and animals, and in 1940 "Bear Hill" was closed despite its popularity as a visitor attraction.

Deprived of their accustomed food supply, the park's bears began frequenting visitor accommodations in search of food. In 1947 the park began regular evening garbage collection, which reduced but did not eliminate the problem. During the 1950s rangers experimented with bearproof garbage containers and education programs aimed at campers, but they also destroyed bears that posed repeated problems—61 of them between 1959 and 1961.

Bears are still destroyed occasionally, but in nowhere near the same numbers. Bearproof lockers are provided and their use required in developed campgrounds and the most heavily used backcountry sites. Park regulations are strict about proper food storage. Still, problems occur. It is best to remember that although they look harmless, the park's bears are wild and powerful animals, capable of tearing open a car to get at an ice chest or severely injuring a person who gets too close. They should be regarded with the same degree of appreciation and respect accorded a roaring river, a precipitous slope or any other beautiful but potentially dangerous park feature.

Facilities

Although Sequoia and Kings Canyon national parks have been administered jointly since 1943, they have distinct characters. This is true not only of their natural features, but also of the development that human stewardship has brought.

Of the two, Kings Canyon is by far the more primitive. The primary road reaches a mere 8.5 miles into the main body of the park, dead-ending along the banks of the South Fork Kings River a few miles past Cedar Grove. A small, separate part of the park surrounding Grant Grove is also accessible by road, and is the location of most of the visitor facilities. The remainder of the park's vast area can be reached only by trail. For the most part Kings Canyon remains true to its inspiration as a wilderness preserve, a rugged mountain fastness where humans are only visitors, not permanent tenants.

Sequoia also contains much wilderness reachable only by trail, but its western slopes are traversed by the Generals Highway, 35 miles of twisting, scenic roadway that climbs from the foothills into the sequoia belt. Leading past many of the park's most famous features, it carries visitors to campgrounds, stores, lodges, picnic areas and numerous pullouts and parking areas between Ash Mountain Park Headquarters and Grant Grove in Kings Canyon National Park.

Roads

Access to the parks is by State Highway 198 from Visalia, 35 miles west of Ash Mountain, or Highway 180 from Fresno, 65 miles west of Grant Grove. Highway 180, which extends into the Cedar Grove area of Kings Canyon, is closed in winter due to falling rock just past the turnoff to Hume Lake. Highway 198 is kept open as far as Giant Forest. The Generals Highway between Giant Forest and Grant Grove is frequently closed for days or weeks at a time by heavy snowfall in winter, a season that varies in length from year to year but usually starts in mid-November and ends by May.

Two other roads also enter the southern end of Sequoia National Park. The Mineral King road is a tortuous track that creeps for 25 miles along an old wagon route from Highway 198 into Mineral King Valley. Much of the road is unpaved, and it takes more than an hour to drive. It is open only in summer. South Fork Drive parallels the South Fork Kaweah River for 12 miles eastward from Highway 198. Also unpaved for part of its length, the narrow road ends at South Fork campground and a small ranger station—closed in winter—just inside the park. Although the campground is open in winter, there is no piped drinking water available then and the road may be too muddy to drive.

The entrance fee, collected at the Big Stump, Ash Mountain and Mineral King entrances to the parks, is $5 (1992), and is good for seven consecutive days. Free Golden Age passes to the national parks are available for those 62 and older who are U.S. citizens or permanent residents. Annual passes to the park are $15, and a Golden Eagle Passport, good for unlimited entry to all elements of the national park system during a calendar year, is $25.

Visitor Centers

Visitor centers are located at Lodgepole, Ash Mountain, Cedar Grove and Grant Grove. All but Cedar Grove are open daily year-round, although hours of operation are shortened in winter. The centers offer books, maps, information, backcountry permits and exhibits.

Campgrounds

Sequoia National Park contains the following campgrounds, listed alphabetically:

Atwell Mill: 6 miles west of Mineral King Ranger Station on Mineral King Road. Elevation 6650 feet. 23 sites. Pit toilets. No reservations. No trailers. Fee $5 per night. Closed in winter.

Buckeye Flat: 1 mile from Hospital Rock picnic area—which is 6 miles from the Ash Mountain entrance—via a side road from Generals Highway. Elevation 2800 feet. 28 sites. No trailers or recreational vehicles. Water, restrooms available. No reservations. Fee $8 per night. Closed in winter.

Cold Springs: A quarter mile west of Mineral King Ranger Station. Elevation 7500 feet. 37 sites. Pit toilets. Water. No trailers. No reservations. Fee $5 per night. Closed in winter.

Dorst: On Generals Highway, 12 miles north of Giant Forest Village. Elevation 6800 feet. 218 sites. Water, restrooms. Fee $8 per night. Closed in winter.

Lodgepole: On Generals Highway, 4 miles north of Giant Forest Village. Elevation 6700 feet. 260 sites. Water, restrooms available. Fee $10 per night. Reservations available during summer. Open year-round, although facilities are reduced in winter. No fee charged after significant snowfall.

Potwisha: 4 miles north of Ash Mountain park entrance. Elevation 2100 feet. 44 sites. Water, restrooms. Dump station. No reservations. Fee $8 per night. Open year-round.

South Fork: 13 miles east of Highway 198 via South Fork Drive from Hammond. 13 sites. Pit toilets. Not recommended for trailers or RV's. No reservations. Open year-round, but water is shut off in winter and unpaved road may be impassable.

Kings Canyon contains the following campgrounds:

Azalea: A quarter mile north of Grant Grove Village on Grant Tree Road. Elevation 6500 feet. 118 sites. Water, restrooms. Dump station. No reservations. Fee $8 per night. Open year-round.

Canyon View: On Highway 180, ½ mile east of the Cedar Grove Village road junction. Elevation 4600 feet. 37 sites. Water, restrooms. Group reservations by mail. Fee $8 per night. Closed in winter.

Crystal Springs: A quarter mile north of Grant Grove Village. Elevation 6500 feet. 67 sites. Water, restrooms. Fee $8 per night. Closed in winter. No reservations.

Moraine: 1 mile east of Cedar Grove Village road junction. Elevation 4600 feet. 120 sites. Water, restrooms. Fee $8 per night. No reservations. Closed in winter.

Sentinel: A quarter mile west of Cedar Grove Village, next to ranger station. Elevation 4600 feet. 83 sites. Water, restrooms. Fee $8 per night. No reservations. Closed in winter.

Sheep Creek: On Highway 180, 1 mile west of Cedar Grove Village. Elevation 4600 feet. 111 sites. Water, restrooms, dump station. Fee $8 per night. No reservations. Closed in winter.

Camping is also available outside the park in Sequoia National Forest. On weekends and holidays, when all the park campgrounds are often filled, the more rustic sites operated by the Forest Service may be the camper's only bet. They generally offer tables and fire rings, as well as pit toilets, but water is often not available or must be drawn from a stream and purified. Usually there is no fee.

Such campgrounds are at Buck Rock and Big Meadows along the signed Forest Service road that meets the east side of Generals Highway about 6 miles south of the junction with Highway 180; Tenmile and Landslide, along the Hume Lake Road from Quail Flat on Generals Highway; and Princess, off Highway 180 between Grant Grove and Hume Lake.

Developed Forest Service campgrounds, where fees are charged and improvements are more reliable, are near the parks at Stony Creek, along Generals Highway just north of the Sequoia National Park boundary, and at Hume Lake, a developed resort area.

On many summer weekends, especially holidays, even the Forest Service campgrounds are likely to be filled. Yet all is not lost. The forest is penetrated by miles of unimproved roads, a legacy of logging activities, and many of them can be safely driven by passenger cars with good clearance. Camping is allowed virtually anywhere in the national forest, as long as you're prepared to provide your own water and to clean up after yourself, and don't mind the lack of such amenities as toilets and tables. Fires are prohibited outside of developed campgrounds unless you obtain a campfire permit, available from any Forest Service office. Those offices also sell National Forest maps, which show logging roads and are essential for travel off the main highways. During times of extreme fire danger, the Forest Service may prohibit all fires outside developed campgrounds.

Food, Gas and Lodging

Guest lodges are operated in the parks by private concessionaires, which pay a percentage of their income to the federal government in exchange for the privilege. Despite efforts by several park managers to remove commercial developments from such scenic and fragile areas as the Giant Forest sequoia grove, the popularity of the shops and guest cabins, as well as the political clout of the operators, stymied them for many years. As a result, parts of the parks retain a resortlike flavor, to the consternation of some and the gratitude of others.

Change is coming, though. Some guest facilities are being moved to a new area north of Lodgepole, which was under construction at the time this was written, but the process is expected to take several years.

In the meantime, lodges are operated at Giant Forest, Grant Grove and Cedar Grove. Giant Forest Lodge offers motel rooms, rustic cabins and housekeeping cabins, and is open all year. Grant Grove Lodge, in Grant Grove Village, offers cabins with baths and housekeeping cabins. It is open year-round. Cedar Grove Lodge offers motel rooms, and closes for the winter.

Gas stations are at Lodgepole, Grant Grove and Cedar Grove. Gift shops are located in Giant Forest Village, Grant Grove and Cedar Grove. Laundromats are operated at Lodgepole and Cedar Grove. Markets are located at Lodgepole, Giant Forest, Grant Grove and Cedar Grove. Showers may be found at Grant Grove Lodge and the Cedar Grove Chevron station. All Cedar Grove facilities close for the winter.

Outside the parks in Sequoia National Forest, privately operated facilities include Montecito-Sequoia Lodge, 9 miles south of Grant Grove on Generals Highway, offering cabins, meals and recreational activities year-round; Kings Canyon Lodge, 17 miles east of Grant Grove on Highway 180, which offers gas, meals and cabins in summer only; and Stony Creek, which offers a lodge, market and coffee shop near the Stony Creek Campground on Generals Highway, also open only in summer.

Other Attractions

Not all of the park's scenic features consist of soaring peaks and tall trees. Treasures are to be found below ground as well. There are more than 100 known caves in Sequoia and Kings Canyon national parks, and although most are open to exploration only by experienced spelunkers, there are two in or near the parks that offer regular tours to more casual visitors.

Crystal Cave is at the end of a narrow, twisting road that leaves Generals Highway near Giant Forest Village. The 6-mile drive takes about 45 minutes, the road is closed to trailers, recreational vehicles and buses, and the weight limit is 6,000 pounds.

The cave, carved in a pocket of marble by seeping water, is operated by the nonprofit Sequoia Natural History Association and is open only in summer. Guided tours of the cavern, which features stalactites, stalagmites, several large chambers and a running underground stream, begin every hour from 10 a.m. to 3 p.m. daily in spring and fall, every half-hour in July and August, and last about 50 minutes. Admission is $3 for adults and $1.50 for kids 11 and under. Sturdy shoes are a must, as is warm clothing—the cave maintains a constant temperature of 48 degrees. Strollers and backpacks are not allowed, and the cave is not accessible to wheelchairs.

Boyden Cavern, privately operated, is located in Sequoia National Forest 22 miles east of Grant Grove on Highway 180. Its features are similar to those of Crystal Cave, and it is likewise open only in summer. Daily tours begin hourly from 10 a.m. to 5 p.m. Admission is $5 for adults and $2.50 for children 12 and under.

Permits, Phone Numbers and Addresses

Although visitors are free to hike anywhere at any time, backpackers who plan to spend the night in the park backcountry need to obtain backcountry use permits. They are free, but limited in number. The system allows park management to control the amount of use that the fragile landscape receives, which is good news for high-mountain meadows but bad news for the spur-of-the-moment traveler who shows up at a popular trailhead on a Saturday morning and finds that its quota has been filled.

About one third of the permits for each trailhead are made available daily on first-come, first-served basis, and may be obtained in person at the parks' visitor centers and ranger stations. The remainder may be reserved by mail if the application is sent at least 14 days before the intended departure date, by writing to:

Sequoia-Kings Canyon National Parks
Three Rivers, CA 93271

Include your dates of departure and return, starting trailhead and ending trailhead, number of people in the party, and at least two alternative trailheads or dates. A recorded backpacking information line may be reached by dialing (209) 565-3708.

For recorded weather and road information, call (209) 565-3351. The tape, updated each morning at about 9, includes information on campground and road closures and conditions, previous day's maximum and minimum temperatures, and the forecast for the next few days.

Reservations for Lodgepole Campground in Sequoia National Park may be made by phone through DESTINET at (800) 436-7275. It will save time if you have all the necessary information at hand before dialing. That includes the number of people in your group, first, second and third choices of arrival date and number of nights, type of camping equipment you will be using, and a Visa or MasterCard number and expiration date.

For general information about Sequoia and Kings Canyon, call (209) 565-3134 between 8 A.M. and 4:30 P.M.

To make reservations for hotel rooms or cabins at the privately operated lodges at Grant Grove, Cedar Grove, Stony Creek and Giant Forest, call (209) 561-3314.

For reservations at the private lodges in Sequoia National Forest, call (800) 227-9900 (Montecito-Sequoia Lodge) or (209) 335-2405 (Kings Canyon Lodge).

For Sequoia National Forest information or campfire permits, contact any of the following:

Supervisor's Office
Sequoia National Forest
900 W. Grand Ave.
Porterville, CA 93257
(209) 784-1500

Hume Lake Ranger District
36273 E. Kings Canyon Road
Dunlap, CA 93621
(209) 338-2251

Tule River Ranger District
32588 Highway 190
Porterville, CA 93257
(209) 539-2607

Hot Springs Ranger District
Route 4, Box 548
California Hot Springs, CA 93207
(805) 548-6503

Greenhorn Ranger District
Federal Building, Room 322
800 Truxton Ave,
Bakersfield, CA 93301
(805) 861-4212

Cannell Meadow Ranger District
P.O. Box 6
Kernville, CA 93238
(619) 376-3781   ■

Monarch Divide in Kings Canyon National Park

Day Hikes in
Sequoia and Kings Canyon

Trails of Cedar Grove

Cedar Grove lies in the heart of Kings Canyon, which naturalist John Muir described as rivaling Yosemite in beauty and grandeur. And although it lacks the spectacular hanging waterfalls that so distinguish Yosemite from other Sierran valleys, Kings Canyon is no less stunning in its depth and the sheer pitch of its ice-carved granite walls. For motorists there is only one way in: Highway 180, which winds 31 tortuous miles from Grant Grove, near the park's Big Stump Entrance Station, down into the deep canyon. Allow at least an hour to drive it. At Cedar Grove, the center of visitor activities in the canyon, you will find a store, lodge, visitor center, ranger station and campgrounds. See the chapter "Facilities" for more details.

Hikes in the Cedar Grove area range from easy jaunts alongside the South Fork Kings River to strenuous climbs up the steep canyon walls. Because of its relatively low elevation, the canyon floor can be extremely warm in summer, so most hikes are best started early in the day. ∎

Hike #1: Bubbs Creek

Distance	5 miles
Level of difficulty	Easy
Child rating	5 and up
Starting elevation	5035 feet
Highest point on trail	5100 feet
Topographic maps	The Sphinx 7.5'; Marion Peak 15'
Guidebook map	1

This easy loop trail serves as a good introduction to the scenery of the Cedar Grove area, offering views of towering, glacier-scoured cliffs and limpid river pools. The trailhead is at Roads End, 6 miles east of Cedar Grove Village on Highway 180, where the only highway into Kings Canyon National Park comes to a dead end, stymied by the sheer valley headwall.

Park in the first lot and look for the sign denoting the trailhead on the south side of the parking area. Water is available near the information booth at the east end of the lot, and restrooms are across the road to the north.

The trail leads south through dense forest, climbs over a small ridge and crosses the South Fork Kings River on a sturdy bridge. Below, the river forms deep, emerald-green pools popular with anglers and, on hot summer days, swimmers willing to brave the chilly waters. On the other side of the river the trail forks, the right fork leading to Zumwalt Meadow and beyond. Take the left branch.

Your trail winds down through some boulders and begins paralleling the river through dense forest. In some spots trail crews blasted through the granite, and remnants of the holes drilled for the dynamite are occasionally visible in the fragments.

At 1 mile the forest thins. Enormous boulders dot the flat alongside the river, and the trail winds near the bottom of the scarred cliffs that form a flank of Avalanche Peak. At 1.6 miles the trail passes through a mess of downed trees, all pointing in the same direction—evidence of the violent forces that gave the peak its name. At 2 miles we reach Avalanche Creek, which flows across the path in several channels and requires early-season hikers to do some boulder hopping to avoid getting wet.

At 2.7 miles we reach a trail junction. The right fork continues out of the valley along an old Indian trade route up the Bubbs Creek drainage. Taking the left fork, we cross the South Fork Kings River on Bailey Bridge and reach another trail junction. The right fork leads to Mist Falls on the Paradise Valley Trail. The left fork returns to Roads End 2 miles away, and it is the path we take.

For the first ½ mile after the bridge, the trail passes through a moist, shady realm of dense foliage, marshy pools, grasses and ferns, as well as hungry mosquitoes (don't forget the repellent). Winding among house-sized boulders, it follows a mostly level route.

The final 1.5 miles of the hike lead though a sparse forest composed primarily of incense-cedar. The route is sunny and hot from mid-morning on, with shade-shunning manzanita and lupine occupying the sandy, open spaces. Huge boulders detached from the soaring granite cliffs lie scattered about the valley's flat floor, legacies of the erosional forces that shaped Kings Canyon.

Finally the trail crosses Copper Creek on a pair of small bridges and reaches the Roads End parking area on the east side, next to a small wooden building where rangers distribute wilderness permits and backcountry information in the summer. ■

Bubbs Creek

Hike #2: Lower Tent Meadow

Distance	7 miles
Level of difficulty	Strenuous
Child rating	10 and up
Starting elevation	5035 feet
Highest point on trail	7825 feet
Topographic maps	The Sphinx 7.5'; Marion Peak 15'
Guidebook map	1

The Copper Creek Trail to Lower Tent Meadow is the toughest day hike out of Cedar Grove. But if you like panoramic views of soaring, snow-capped peaks and yawning, ice-carved canyons, it can't be matched.

The trailhead is at Roads End. Drive around the highway loop to the second parking area, where the Copper Creek Trail sign stands. Water and restrooms are nearby.

The well-engineered trail switchbacks steeply up the flank of North Dome, passing at first through scattered Jeffrey pines and then across an open slope clothed in manzanita and stunted oak. The southern exposure makes this a hot, thirsty ascent in the afternoon, so it is better tackled early in the day.

At 1 mile the trail re-enters forest cover, and the needle-cushioned path offers a welcome respite from the gravel and sand of the introductory stages of the hike. Back to the south are broad views of the crags, domes and deeply carved tributary canyons at the east end of Kings Canyon. The vista will change and grow even more spectacular as the trail gains elevation, eventually unfolding to include the 12,000-foot peaks of the Sphinx Crest to the southeast.

The trail continues to climb, but at 1.3 miles the switchbacks end and the route then goes nearly due north, into the gradually widening canyon of Copper Creek, which lies invisible and unheard some 800 feet below. At 1.8 miles the moderately ascending trail crosses a small stream, bedecked with wildflowers and jewellike butterflies, and then climbs a little more steeply. At 2 miles we enter thick forest at 6800 feet, the realm of cedar, sugar pine and white fir.

The abundance of water on this slope has allowed the trees to grow to magnificent size. The trail continues in their dense shade for about a mile, breaking into the open at 3.1 miles, where a slope apparently cleared by avalanches supports a stand of quaking aspen. Past the gleaming white trunks and dancing foliage of these beautiful trees, the trail continues a brief climb and arrives at Lower Tent Meadow at 3.5 miles.

The spot identified as the meadow isn't much more than a patch of nearly level ground on the hillside, near an unnamed tributary of Copper Creek. The small stream is lined with aspens, and several informal campsites are scattered about.

There is one well-established site, which contains a bear-proof steel locker for food storage. Lower Tent Meadow is a popular stopping point for backpackers heading into the Granite Basin and Monarch Divide area to the north, which also makes it popular with panhandling members of the black-bear clan.

After a lunch break and a refreshing foot bath in the icy stream, follow the trail back, stopping plenty of times to offset the bone-jarring impact of the long descent.   ■

Aspens at Lower Tent Meadow

Hike #3: Cedar Grove Overlook

Distance	Overlook 5 miles;
	Lewis Creek loop 8 miles
Level of difficulty	Strenuous
Child rating	10 and up
Starting elevation	4680 feet
Highest point on trail	6200 feet
Topographic maps	Cedar Grove 7.5'; Marion Peak 15'
Guidebook map	3

Cedar Grove is at the bottom of one of the deepest canyons in North America, so it should come as no surprise that nearly every trail in the area goes uphill. Nature, however, rewards those willing to sweat and gasp by presenting them with the most sublime views.

The overlook trail is no exception. Although it's the steepest of Cedar Grove's trails, it also offers the best views of Kings Canyon, a reward certainly commensurate with the effort required.

The trailhead is near Cedar Grove Village at the foot of the canyon's north wall. To reach it follow the village road across the bridge over the South Fork Kings River, and ¼ mile past the market to the pack-station parking area. A sign announces the Hotel Creek trailhead. Fill your water bottles beforehand; there is no faucet at the parking area, and the hot, dusty trail induces a powerful thirst.

The sign also warns that the brush lining the initial two miles of trail is known to harbor deer ticks, which can carry Lyme disease. This debilitating illness first causes flulike symptoms of nausea, aches and fever. Later stages can cause arthritis, meningitis and neurological damage. There is no good treatment, so authorities emphasize prevention. Stay out of the brush, wear long sleeves and trousers if possible, and examine yourself thoroughly afterward for the ticks, which are scarcely ⅛" wide. Generally you have 12 hours to remove a tick before it infects you through its bite, which produces a characteristic rash.

The disease is relatively rare, and only one case is known to have been contracted in Sequoia and Kings Canyon national parks. The safest procedure is simply to remain on the trail when passing through brushy areas, especially in the foothills.

With that cheery warning in mind, we ignore the trail on the left and begin our steep, switchbacking ascent of the canyon wall. The trail first climbs through oak and scattered pines along the course of Hotel Creek. After ½ mile, the trees drop away and the open slope is clothed in manzanita and other members of the chaparral plant community. This part of the trail is extremely hot from midday on, and is best tackled in the early morning.

Your hard work is soon rewarded with views up and down Kings Canyon. Across the canyon are Lookout Peak, Sentinel Dome and Avalanche Peak. Below are the river and the campgrounds, roads and other facilities of the Cedar Grove area.

The switchbacks end at about 1.8 miles, as the trail enters a forest of ponderosa and Jeffrey pine and leads west. At 2.2 miles the trail forks, the left branch dipping and then climbing on its way to the overlook 0.3 mile away. The viewpoint, a knob of granite protruding from the southwest tip of the ridge, offers grand views that stretch from the valley's east end and the canyon of Bubbs Creek to the foothills in the west where the Kings River leaves the mountains. Looking to the north you can see the snow-topped peaks of the Monarch Divide arcing around the headwaters of small Lewis Creek.

Upon returning to the trail junction, you have a choice: return the way you came to complete a 5-mile trip, or proceed along the other fork to Lewis Creek and go downhill for an 8-mile loop.

If you choose the latter, your route will proceed north through an open forest of snags and fire-scarred yellow pines. This area was burned in the Lewis Creek fire of 1980, and although the damaged forest now offers little shade for hikers, it provides a demonstration of how an ecosystem heals itself from the wounds of wildfire. Already, sun-loving plants such as manzanita, mountain misery, lupine and paintbrush thickly cover the blackened wreckage of fallen pines, and near those trees that survived the blaze, seedlings sprout from the soil. The long process of rebuilding the forest is under way.

Half a mile from the junction the trail climbs briefly and then heads downhill. At 4.5 miles it reaches a junction, the right fork leading up the Lewis Creek drainage to Frypan Meadow. We take the left, which curves around to the south and descends, steeply at times, passing uneventfully through more fire-scarred forest to the Lewis Creek trailhead and parking area. At the trailhead turn left and follow the road—or the slightly less level trail—back to your car 1.5 miles away.   ■

Looking east from Cedar Grove Overlook

Hike #4: Mist Falls

Distance	8 miles
Level of difficulty	Moderate
Child rating	10 years and up
Starting elevation	5035 feet
Highest point on trail	5660 feet
Topographic maps	The Sphinx 7.5'; Marion Peak 15'
Guidebook map	1

Early summer is the best time to travel this popular trail, which leads hikers out of Kings Canyon along the South Fork Kings River. When the river is high with snowmelt, it tumbles and roars down its gorge in a spectacular display of musical power, while the falls themselves explode on the rocks and fill the air with spray.

The trail leaves from Roads End. Park in the first lot, where a sign indicates wilderness information is available. The trailhead is at the east end of the lot, next to a small wooden building where overnight hikers can obtain wilderness permits. There is a faucet near the building; pit toilets are on the other side of the road.

The trail crosses Copper Creek on a pair of wooden bridges, and then leads across sandy, level terrain sparsely forested with Jeffrey and ponderosa pines and incense-cedar. Huge boulders detached from the canyon walls lie scattered about, and lupine and manzanita grow in the sunny open spaces. This stretch can be hot on a summer day, so it is best to start early.

After 1.5 miles the trail leads into a shaded, moist area dominated by ferns and mosquitos (until late season). The forest here is much denser, and the path winds closely between gnarled trunks and granite boulders.

At 2 miles you reach a signed junction near the foot of Bailey Bridge. The right fork leads over the bridge and up Bubbs Creek; we take the left fork and climb across a rocky slope. The ascent steepens as the trail traverses the canyonside, rising 70 or 80 feet above the rushing stream. At 3 miles the trail bends near a series of spectacular cataracts and then continues its moderate climb up an open, rocky hillside that provides tremendous views back down the canyon. In the distance you can see the Bubbs Creek canyon leading east out of Kings Canyon, the oddly shaped horn of granite called The Sphinx directly ahead, and the deeply incised bulk of Avalanche Peak to the right of the Sphinx.

Resuming the climb, we soon enter thick forest. Half a mile farther the trail deposits us on the riverbank, 4 miles from the trailhead. From here Mist Falls is visible, thundering into a pool less than 100 yards away.

The falls takes its name from the enormous quantity of spray launched into the air as the water tumbles over the lip of a cliff and slams onto the boulders below. Downstream from the waterfall, the upstream side of every tree and every boulder is slick and moss-grown from windblown mist, which hovers in the air so thickly that it all but obscures the falls. Even on a hot day the flat shoreline near the base of Mist Falls is cool and damp, and you'll want to move out of reach of the spray for a lunch break.

Like most Sierran waterfalls, this one is at its best early in the season when the river is high. By late summer, and in drought years, it loses much of its vigor.

The trail continues past the falls to Paradise Valley, 3 miles distant and a popular stopping point for backpackers on their way to the John Muir Trail and the beautiful country around Rae Lakes.

It is dangerous to climb on the rocks around the waterfall, which are extremely slippery even in late summer when the river is relatively low.

Return the way you came.   ■

Mist Falls live up to their name

Hike #5: Roaring River Falls, via Zumwalt Meadow

Distance	5.8 miles
Level of difficulty	Easy
Child rating	5 and up
Starting elevation	5035 feet
Highest point on trail	5080 feet
Topographic maps	The Sphinx 7.5'; Marion Peak 15'
Guidebook map	2

Roaring River Falls and Zumwalt Meadow can each be reached by a short pathway that leads from a nearby parking lot along Highway 180 between Cedar Grove and Roads End. This hike, however, offers the dual reward of meadow and falls for only a little extra effort, and as a bonus avoids crowds most of the way.

The trailhead is at Roads End. Follow the directions for the first part of Hike #1, but after crossing the South Fork Kings River take the right trail fork, which leads through a field of massive boulders and shattered rock. This debris has fallen or been plucked from Grand Sentinel, the granite monolith that towers nearly 3500 feet above you, during eons of action by ice.

The trail then leads to the edge of the river, passing through thick stands of yellow pine, black oak and incense-cedar, where ferns thrive in the moist shade. At 0.8 mile the trail forks as it reaches the edge of Zumwalt Meadow. Ringed with trees that are slowly beginning to encroach on its thick grass, the meadow was formerly a small lake formed when debris scraped together by the Kings Canyon glacier created a barrier that captured runoff from the nearby cliffs. Such debris forms low ridges called moraines along both sides of the canyon in this area.

Eventually the lake filled with sediment, forming a meadow. This process is common in the Sierra, and in the scattering of trees along the meadow's rim you can see the beginning of the next phase in the former lake's evolution: eventually, it will become forest.

The meadow is named for Daniel K. Zumwalt, a Tulare County lawyer who represented the Southern Pacific Railroad in local matters. Zumwalt appears to have played a role in the formation of General Grant National Park, the predecessor of Kings Canyon National Park. Historians, however, are not clear on exactly what part Zumwalt and the railroad had in the park's creation. There is speculation that Southern Pacific threw its weight behind the bill establishing the park because it would attract visitors who would ride the train to reach the area, and because it would eliminate competition for logging activities on other land owned by the railroad in the southern Sierra.

Contemplating the mysterious motives of politicians and lawyers, we take the right trail fork at the meadow's edge and skirt the north side of the level meadow floor. At 1 mile, we reach a junction with the fork that passed along the south side. Continue to your right. At just over 2 miles, the trail winds through another field of boulders, and then turns south, reaching Roaring River Falls at 2.5 miles.

The waterfall is quite impressive, thundering into a rocky bowl at the base of towering cliffs. From the viewpoint, however, only about 80 feet of the falls can be seen, a third of the total height.

On the way back, stay to the right when the trail divides at the west end of Zumwalt Meadow. This route will take you around the meadow's south side, leading up into the massive jumble of rocks at the base of Grand Sentinel. The views down onto the meadow from the boulder pile are impressive, providing a much different perspective than you enjoyed on the way out. Above the meadow on the other side of the canyon, North Dome rears its bald head nearly 3,700 feet above.

When the trails merge again at the east end of the meadow, continue back the way you came. ■

Roaring River Falls

Hike #6: Sheep Creek

Distance	2 miles
Level of difficulty	Moderate
Child rating	3 and up
Starting elevation	4600 feet
Highest point on trail	5200
Topographic maps	Cedar Grove 7.5'; Marion Peak 15'
Guidebook map	3

This short hike on the Don Cecil trail leads uphill a mile to a bridge crossing Sheep Creek, a small stream that cascades pleasantly from one fern-lined pool to the next. Named by sheepherders who once camped in the area, devastating the native vegetation with their voracious flocks, it serves as the water supply for Cedar Grove, so wading or otherwise contaminating it is strictly forbidden. Still, even if you can't use it for a refreshing dip, it serves as a nice destination for a leisurely walk.

The signed trailhead is on the south side of the road, about ¼ mile east of the turnoff to Cedar Grove Village on Highway 180. A connecting trail can also be followed out of the Sentinel Campground, near the ranger station, where water and restrooms are located.

Your broad path ascends moderately through incense cedar, white fir and oak. The low, dense ground cover with small white flowers is mountain misery, also known as bear clover and kit-kit-dizze. The fernlike leaves and woody stems are resinous, and they become sticky on warm days, a feature which led early settlers who walked through it to rue the experience and to coin the misery name. It was called kit-kit-dizze by the Miwok Indians of the central and northern Sierra Nevada, who made a tea from the leaves and drank it as a cure for several diseases.

About midway to the stream crossing, just after you cross a dirt road leading to a Forest Service heliport, the trail begins offering good views of the crest of the Monarch Divide, back across Kings Canyon to the north. The barren crags of the divide separate the drainages of the Middle and South forks of the Kings River.

At 1 mile the trail crosses Sheep Creek. It is possible to clamber around some boulders and continue upstream a short distance, to a pleasant spot to sit by the water and savor the song of a nearby cascade as it drops into a cool, shaded grotto of stone.

From here the Don Cecil Trail continues to Lookout Peak, 5.5 steep miles beyond, and out of the park to Summit Meadow.

Return the way you came.   ■

Hike #7: Sphinx Creek

Distance	10 miles
Level of difficulty	Strenuous
Child rating	10 and up
Starting elevation	5035 feet
Highest point on trail	6240 feet
Topographic maps	The Sphinx 7.5'; Marion Peak 15'
Guidebook map	1

On the way to Sphinx Creek, which takes its name from the oddly shaped stone pinnacle on the south canyon wall above Bubbs Creek, hikers follow the route of an old Indian trail out of Kings Canyon. The trail served as an avenue of trade between inhabitants of the western slopes of the Sierra in the Sequoia-Kings Canyon area and the linguistically related tribes living in the Owens Valley on the east side of the range. The route, later used by white explorers and settlers, followed the Bubbs Creek drainage to climb over 12,000-foot Kearsarge Pass, and surveys have revealed evidence of numerous camps along the way.

The trail begins at Roads End, and for the first 2.7 miles follows the route described at the start of Hike #1. At the trail junction ¼ mile past Avalanche Creek, where the left branch leads across Bailey Bridge and back to Roads End, take the right fork instead.

The trail leads over a series of four bridges crossing many-channeled Bubbs Creek. Almost immediately beyond, the trail begins to switchback up the east wall of Kings Canyon. The climb is steep at times, and the path is dusty. Along the slope, oak trees and pinyon pines—rare on this side of the Sierra—frame increasingly panoramic views of the canyon below and Paradise Valley to the north.

Pinyon pines are more common on the drier east side of the mountains, where they occupy the upper sagebrush belt along with Utah juniper and mountain mahogany. The cones contain edible nuts, which formed a staple in the diet of the Owens Valley Paiutes, who shared common ancestors with the Monache of the Sequoia-Kings Canyon area. On the west slope, pine nuts were obtained primarily through trade in limited quantities, and the far more common acorn formed the staple element of the diet.

At 4 miles and 6000 feet the switchbacks end, as the trail enters the canyon of Bubbs Creek and then proceeds nearly due east. The climb is more moderate now, and the path lies close to the lovely stream, which drops in a series of pools and cascades. At 5 miles the trail reaches Sphinx Creek and the first legal campsites since the Kings Canyon floor.

The trail continues up the canyon, eventually meeting the famous John Muir Trail in Vidette Meadow, at the base of Kearsarge Pinnacles. East of Sphinx

Creek, the canyon shows the lingering effects of a fire that swept through the area in the 1970s, destroying most of the trees. Today, charred snags stand above dense stands of manzanita and blue elderberry, which have flourished in the cleared areas. But pockets of mature trees survived the flames, and in their shade sprout the seedlngs that will someday reclaim the area.

A stroll upstream is rewarding, and the climb is not severe. As a bonus for those who tarry, Bubbs Creek offers fine fishing.

Return the way you came.   ■

The Sphinx, from the Mist Falls Trail

Trails of the foothills

In winter and spring, deep snow covers the high country of Sequoia and Kings Canyon. Although campgrounds remain open year-round at upper-elevation Lodgepole and Grant Grove, the trails are buried and the forests become the province of skiers and snowshoers.

Hiking opportunities may still be found in the foothills to the south and west of the Giant Forest. In summer these low-elevation trails are far too hot for pleasant hiking, but in winter and spring the hillsides are carpeted with flowers, the grass is yet green, and the temperatures are moderate.

Winter hiking in the foothills is a vastly different experience from summer travel in the evergreen forests at higher elevations. The predominant foothill plants are oak trees, grasses and chaparral—a tough, drought-resistant community of woody bushes and shrubs such as manzanita, chamise and ceanothus. Shade is scarce, and streams are uncommon. The foothills are also home to the most unlikable residents of the parks: ticks, poison oak and rattlesnakes, none of which are common above 5,000 feet.

Ticks are quite numerous in the foothills, and several varieties carry disease. They lie in wait on grass stems or the branches of shrubs, and become attached to the arms or legs of passing hikers as they brush against them. They crawl upward, and eventually attach themselves to the skin, biting and sucking blood. It is a good idea to wear long-sleeved shirts and trousers when hiking in the foothills, no matter how hot it is. Stop every few minutes and brush off any ticks that you've picked up, before they can become attached. At the end of the day, conduct a thorough examination to make sure none made it inside your clothes. If you are bitten, use a pair of tweezers to grasp the tick near the head and pull it out, making sure not to crush it or leave any part of it embedded in the skin. If a rash develops around the site of a bite, or you are unable to remove the entire tick, see a doctor.

In spring and summer poison oak may be recognized by its clusters of shiny green leaves, which have a slightly oily appearance and grow in groups of three. During winter, however, the branches are bare, or carry only small, reddish new leaves, and are harder to identify. Contact with any part of the plant will produce blisters that itch maddeningly. Be on the lookout for it, especially in moister areas near streams and in the shade of oak trees. Again, long pants and sleeves help prevent contact. Washing with strong soap at the end of a hiking day removes the plant's irritating oils and may prevent the rash from developing. If the blisters do develop, any over-the-counter cream containing hydrocortisone will provide relief.

Rattlesnakes are common in the foothills, often basking in sunlight on trails when it is cold, or seeking the shade of rocks and brush during hot weather.

Rattlesnake bites are extremely rare, however, and hardly ever fatal. The venomous creatures can usually be avoided by the simple precautions of keeping your eyes on the trail ahead, staying out of thick underbrush, and never putting hands or feet anywhere you can't see. Given the opportunity, a rattlesnake will avoid human beings, striking only when surprised or threatened.

Despite its drawbacks, foothill hiking offers one of the few alternatives for those who want to stretch their legs during the months of winter and early spring. The following three hikes offer a taste of several types of foothill terrain and plant communities. They originate in the general vicinity of Potwisha Campground, which is open year-round and is situated about 4 miles beyond the Ash Mountain park entrance on Highway 198. ■

Hike #8: Marble Falls

Distance	7 miles
Level of difficulty	Strenuous
Child rating	10 and up
Starting elevation	2120 feet
Highest point on trail	3600 feet
Topographic maps	Giant Forest 7.5'; Giant Forest 15'
Guidebook map	4

The trail to Marble Falls parallels the course of the Marble Fork Kaweah River, which originates in Giant Forest and descends along a rocky course south to join the Kaweah River. The trailhead is next to campsite 16 in Potwisha Campground.

Follow the dirt road for about 100 yards until it crosses the concrete channel of the Southern California Edison Co. flume. The trail leaves the road just past the wooden bridge. Keep an eye out for the wooden trail sign on your right, directly across the road from the fenced-in water gate used to control the flow in the flume.

The trail climbs steeply up the hillside, switchbacking through a dense stand of oaks. In their shade grow ferns and thick banks of miner's lettuce, with its tiny white flowers and fleshy, edible leaves. At 0.8 mile the switchbacks stop and the trail proceeds moderately upslope into the north-south canyon of the Marble Fork.

At 1.2 miles the trail emerges from the trees and leads through dense chaparral. The hardy shrubs of this common foothill plant community—which derives its name from the Spanish word for scrub oak, *chaparro*—are well-adapted to heat and drought, and can survive the wildfires that frequently sweep across the dry foothill slopes.

The trail steepens at 1.6 miles and becomes extremely narrow. Here the canyon walls drop precipitously to the river, some 600 feet below, and great care must be taken to avoid slipping or stumbling on the loose rock underfoot.

The trail occasionally levels out, but only temporarily, always resuming its moderate climb. Near the falls—actually a series of cascades—the trail crosses outcroppings of marble, created when ancient limestone sediments were subjected to the intense heat and pressure that attended the formation of the Sierra range. Similar bands of marble occur in several areas of the park.

The trail reaches the river's edge at 3.5 miles. Travel up or downstream is dangerous and should be attempted only by experienced cross-country travelers. Be careful near the water, which in spring is fast-moving and powerful.

Return the way you came.   ■

Hike #9: Middle Fork Loop

Distance	1 mile
Level of difficulty	Easy
Child rating	3 and up
Starting elevation	2120 feet
Highest point on trail	2160 feet
Topographic maps	Giant Forest 7.5'; Giant Forest 15'
Guidebook map	4

Potwisha Campground is named after the subgroup of Monache Indians who occupied the foothills in the Kaweah River drainage. This easy trail leads along the bank of the Middle Fork Kaweah River through what once was the site of a Potwisha village. Along the way it passes pictographs and bedrock mortars

The trailhead is directly across Generals Highway from the entrance to Potwisha Campground. Follow the paved road into the recreational-vehicle dump station, and bear right, following the pavement to the end. The path begins next to a sign that says "Use restroom in campground."

The trail hugs the bank of the Middle Fork, leading upstream. After about 50 yards, it crosses a large patch of exposed granite, which slopes down toward the stream and commands a pleasing view of its many pools. This granite is pocked by numerous bedrock mortars, cuplike depressions ground into its surface and used by Indian women to pulverize acorns and other nuts and seeds. The village site lies under the RV dump station.

The trail leads across the granite and descends to the sand-and-boulder-strewn flat alongside the river. A few yards past the bedrock mortars, look up to your left. Several pictographs are painted on the large overhanging boulder atop the riverbank, facing the water.

The meaning of the drawings is unclear. Similar pictographs are found in several sites in Sequoia and Kings Canyon, including Hospital Rock, just 2 miles east of Potwisha Campground along Generals Highway; Tehipite Valley in Kings Canyon; and near Volcano Falls, just outside the southern boundary of Sequoia. The latter two are inaccessible except to hikers. The Hospital Rock and Potwisha pictographs are the most spectacular.

The trail continues past the pictographs to the base of a wooden bridge over the Middle Fork, which provides access to the Southern California Edison Co. flume on the other side. At the bridge, turn left and follow the trail up a steep but short hill. At the top of the hill, the trail reaches a junction. To the right, the path leads to Hospital Rock picnic area, 2.5 miles away. Turn left, following the trail downhill, through a pleasant oak woodland, back to the RV dump station. ■

Hike #10: Paradise Creek

Distance	3.2 miles
Level of difficulty	Moderate
Child rating	5 and up
Starting elevation	2720 feet
Highest point on trail	3280 feet
Topographic maps	Giant Forest 7.5'; Giant Forest 15'
Guidebook map	4

Paradise Creek is an oasis amid the arid, sun-scorched hillsides of the Kaweah River drainage. This trail, which at one time extended from the Middle Fork Kaweah River south to Atwell Grove and Mineral King Valley, is now maintained for only a small part of that distance.

To reach the trailhead, drive to the Hospital Rock picnic area, about 6 miles east of the Ash Mountain park entrance on the Generals Highway. Hospital Rock was the site of the largest known Potwisha village, and interpretive displays at the picnic area provide information about the Indians' way of life. The village site itself lies under the picnic area parking lot, but some bedrock mortars have been preserved, and the large boulder from which the site takes its name still bears pictographs. Although much damaged by moisture, they retain their vivid colors.

To reach the Paradise Creek trailhead, cross the Generals Highway from the Hospital Rock picnic area and walk 0.6 mile to the Buckeye Flat campground. The road is closed to vehicles from late autumn until early summer, and in the summer day-use parking is prohibited in the campground. The paved, narrow road climbs moderately before descending to the campground, which is situated on a bench above the Middle Fork.

The trail begins at the south end of the campground, at campsite 25. It climbs gently out of the campground through a thick stand of oak and then descends to a footbridge crossing the middle fork at 0.7 mile. Bear left on the other side of the bridge, passing through thick brush and then emerging on an open hillside next to cascading Paradise Creek.

The trail then climbs away from the creek, entering a drier zone inhabited by manzanita and other drought-tolerant shrubs, interspersed with oak trees. At 1.3 miles ponderosa pines join the woodland community, and the trail is bordered by thick stands of knee-high mountain misery. Level now, the trail again reaches the edge of Paradise Creek at 1.6 miles.

Return the way you came.   ■

Trails of Giant Forest

No area in Sequoia-Kings Canyon national parks draws as many visitors as Giant Forest, and with good reason. There are more extensive stands of giant sequoias elsewhere, but none has the same emotional impact as this 5-square-mile collection of groves and meadows, wherein grow four of the five largest trees on earth, as well as hundreds of equally impressive specimens.

The Giant Forest straddles Generals Highway, about 17 miles north of the Ash Mountain park entrance on Highway 198 from Visalia. For the purposes of this book, the area is considered to extend beyond the perimeter of the Giant Forest grove itself to include the Lodgepole and Dorst areas, which are 4 and 12 miles, respectively, north of Giant Forest Village along Generals Highway.

Be cautious when driving through the Giant Forest area. Many photogenic stands of sequoia are close to the road, and there are numerous pullouts adjacent to popular attractions. Use them. Far too many visitors find themselves so awestruck by the sights that they stop their vehicles in the middle of the highway to gawk, or wander into traffic while intently peering through the viewfinders of their cameras. Pay close attention to the posted limits—park rangers will not hesitate to ticket speeders—keep an eye out for errant pedestrians and oblivious drivers, and take a hike. It's really the best way to appreciate the scenery.

Full visitor services are available at Giant Forest Village and Lodgepole. No camping is allowed within the Giant Forest grove itself, although overnight accommodations are available at Giant Forest Lodge. Campgrounds are at Lodgepole and Dorst. For more details, consult the chapter "Facilities." ■

Hike #11: Hazelwood Nature Trail

Distance	1 mile
Level of difficulty	Easy
Child rating	3 years
Starting elevation	6400 feet
Highest point on trail	6480 feet
Topographic maps	Giant Forest 7.5'; Giant Forest 15'
Guidebook map	5

Visitors looking for a quick and painless introduction to the ecology of the sequoia forest can find precisely what they seek on the Hazelwood Nature Trail, a self-guiding 1-mile loop conveniently located in the heart of the Giant Forest Village area.

The mostly level route, which winds through a majestic stand of sequoias, leads past many interpretive displays. Although your walk will be accompanied by the sounds of traffic making its laborious way along the twisting Generals Highway nearby, the trail will most likely be uncrowded even on a summer weekend. The same is true of virtually every hike in the park, no matter how easy or how close to major attractions—if you are willing to stretch your legs, you'll be rewarded.

The signed Hazelwood trailhead is at a small parking area on the south side of Generals Highway, directly across the road from Giant Forest Lodge. The pathway leads gently uphill along the edge of a moist, grassy area, too small to be properly called a meadow, characteristic of many sequoia groups. The giant trees require enormous amounts of water, and tend to cluster along the edges of such natural drainages. Pioneering Sierra naturalist John Muir was of the opinion that the great trees actually created these small watercourses, rather than the reverse. Writing in *The Yosemite*, he theorized:

> When attention is called to the method of sequoia streammaking, it will be appre- hended at once. The roots of this immense tree fill the ground, forming a thick sponge that absorbs and holds back the rain and melting snow, only allowing it to ooze and flow gently. Indeed, every fallen leaf and rootlet, as well as long clasping root, and prostrate trunk, may be regarded as a dam hoarding the bounty of storm-clouds, and dispensing it as blessings all through the summer, instead of allowing it to go headlong in short-lived floods.

It is apparent that the sequoias favor naturally existing drainages, where water is relatively abundant, for without plentiful moisture they do not survive their first few years. But although they cannot be credited with creating the streams along which they often germinate, the sequoias do spread an amazing net of roots, just as Muir observed, anchoring the forest soil and slowing runoff. The roots typically lie no more than 4 or 5 feet underground but may extend more than 200 feet from the tree, and the entire root system of a mature sequoia may cover 2-4 acres.

Stay to the right at the first trail junction, ¼ mile from the parking area. Signs along the trail, which is well-marked, identify some of the other plants of the Giant Forest area, explain the relationship between fire and sequoia propagation, and present a host of other facts about the birth, life and death of the big trees.

Bear left at the next junction, about 0.3 mile into the walk. The trail crosses the upper end of the grassy area here and continues downhill, passing near the base of several large specimens. Ignore the next two trail spurs leading to the right, which cross the highway and end at Giant Forest Lodge. At the third junction we rejoin the early trail and follow it back to the parking lot and our starting point.   ■

Young female mule deer

Hike #12: Heather Lake

Distance	8.2 miles
Level of difficulty	Strenuous
Child rating	10 and up
Starting elevation	7270 feet
Highest point on trail	9200 feet
Topographic maps	Lodgepole 7.5';
	Triple Divide Peak 15'
Guidebook map	7

Heather Lake is the first of a string of small, picturesque alpine tarns reached by the extremely popular Lakes Trail. Created by the scouring action of glaciers, tarns typically rest in rocky bowls ringed by jagged cliffs, and Heather Lake is no exception.

The trailhead is at the Wolverton parking area, on the left of the parking lot as you drive in from Generals Highway. Restrooms are provided nearby at the picnic area but water is not, so you're better off filling up before you arrive.

Ignoring the Long Meadow loop trail that branches almost immediately to the right past the sign, we head east and begin climbing on top of a gravelly ridge created by the Tokopah Glacier, which scoured the deep valley to our left. This ridge, a lateral moraine, consists of rock, sand and earthen debris scraped together and pushed to one side by the advancing ice mass as it slowly ground away at the granite walls of the valley. The Tokopah Glacier was once more than 500 feet deep, filling the valley of the Marble Fork Kaweah River, and the basin that holds Heather Lake was one of its birthplaces.

The trail climbs and then levels briefly before climbing again, repeating this pattern as it surmounts each of several morainal ridges. To the right, small Wolverton Creek chatters and sings, watering a lush garden of greenery and wildflowers.

At 1.5 miles the climb steepens before crossing an unnamed and unmapped tributary of Wolverton Creek. At 1.8 miles the trail splits, the route to Panther Gap branching to the right. Taking the left fork, we continue our climb, which is steep at times, reaching another fork at 2.1 miles.

At this point the hiker has a decision to make. Both forks lead to Heather Lake, but the routes are very different. To the left lies the Watchtower Trail, the more level of the two, which makes its way along the lip of the Tokopah Valley, clinging to a narrow ledge dynamited out of the granite. It offers great views, especially where it clambers onto the great rock promontory for which it is named, but it is not for the faint of heart. In addition, it may be blocked by snow early or late in the season, and it is sometimes closed—as it was during part of the summer of

1991—so trail crews can remove the avalanche debris that occasionally thunders down from the cliffs above.

The right fork, the Hump Trail, offers less spectacular views and is a great deal steeper than the Watchtower Trail. It is shorter, however, and more reliable, and it lacks precipitous cliffs that might frighten acrophobes. It climbs steeply, switchbacking at times, through thick stands of red fir, reaching the top of the ridge at 3.7 miles. The elevation here is 9,200 feet, and the view to the north, across the gleaming stone headwall of Tokopah Valley to the peaks of the Silliman Crest, is quite picturesque, giving hikers plenty to look at while they catch their breath.

From here the trail drops steeply to rejoin the Watchtower Trail at 4 miles, and then reaches the shore of Heather Lake at 4.1 miles. The lake fills a depression carved out of granite that was easily torn up by the glacier because of the many joints and cracks in it. At the lip of the bowl, holding back the water, is a wall of relatively more resistant granite, which the glacier was unable to remove. Meltwater, first from the receding glacier and now from the snow and ice that collect in the shadows of the surrounding cliffs, keeps the lake filled.

Camping has been prohibited at Heather Lake, which is such a popular destination that an open-air pit-toilet has been installed to keep hikers from fouling the area. This facility is primitive and lacks privacy, but it offers one of the grandest views of any outhouse in the Sierra. Carry your own toilet paper.

The trail continues past Heather Lake to Emerald, Aster and Pear lakes. Heather Lake, however, is the perfect stopping point for a picnic lunch and a leisurely appreciation of the interplay between sky, water and stone that characterizes the High Sierra.

Return the way you came.   ■

Hike #13: Huckleberry Meadow

Distance	4 miles
Level of difficulty	Easy
Child rating	5 years and up
Starting elevation	6400 feet
Highest point on trail	6900 feet
Topographic maps	Giant Forest 7.5'; Giant Forest 15'
Guidebook map	5

The meadows of the Giant Forest are as essential a part of its character as the big trees themselves. In dense forest, surrounded by towering sugar pines and white firs, themselves noteworthy specimens, the giant sequoias lose some of their visual impact. But when seen fringing one of the many verdant meadows, with a rainbow carpet of wildflowers and viridescent grasses lapping at their feet, the ruddy sequoias take on a new aspect.

This easy loop hike leads to one such meadow. Along the way it leads past one of the oldest structures in the park, and also a cluster of bedrock grinding mortars, reminders of the now-vanished people who first called the area home.

The hike begins at the same trailhead as the Hazelwood Nature Trail (Hike #11), and for the first 0.3 mile follows the route of that hike. When you arrive at the second junction, instead of turning left to complete the Hazelwood loop, continue straight ahead for a short distance, past the sign indicating the trail to Bear Hill. Bear Hill was formerly the site of the Sequoia National Park dump, and early in the century the area was a prime attraction for black bears and for crowds of tourists who enjoyed watching them paw through the garbage. At one time rangers even erected bleachers so spectators could enjoy the evening show in greater comfort. The dump was closed in 1940 because of the increasing number of conflicts between bears and humans.

Just past the Bear Hill turnoff, the trail splits again. The right fork follows the Soldiers Trail to Moro Rock; our route lies to the left. The trail begins a gentle ascent, crossing the small trickle of water that gives life to the greenery beneath the sequoias here. At 0.4 mile the trail forks again. Bearing right, we climb up the side of a low ridge through thick undergrowth.

At 0.7 mile the trail reaches the ridgetop and enters a much drier zone, sparsely forested, with an undergrowth of manzanita. The sequoias are absent here, and on a warm afternoon the characteristic vanilla scent of Jeffrey pines fills the air.

At 0.9 mile the trail begins descending and re-enters a moist, shaded realm. Another 0.3 mile brings us to the Squatter's Cabin on the edge of Huckleberry Meadow. The cabin, a rough log structure with split shake roof, was built in the

1880s by a man who attempted to file a claim on the adjoining land only to find that it already belonged to pioneering cattle rancher Hale Tharp.

Throughout spring and summer the meadow is richly carpeted with grasses and a rainbow profusion of wildflowers. To get a closer look, walk out along the top of fallen tree trunks, rather than trampling the delicate plants. Sierran meadows are fragile and do not recover easily or quickly from the damage inflicted by even the casual trampling of hiking boots.

At the meadow's edge the trail divides again. Bear left, paralleling the north fringe of the meadow for a level ¼ mile, and then go left again at the next junction.

The trail climbs gently for the next 0.4 mile, reaching another junction just south of Circle Meadow. Take the left fork, descend a bit and then level out, passing another branch to the right, which leads to the Alta Trail. Continuing left on the Huckleberry Meadow Trail, we cross aspen-lined Little Deer Creek, stay to the left at another junction and reach the bedrock mortars at 2.7 miles.

The mortars lie just to the right of the trail, a half-dozen holes worn into a slab of exposed granite by Indians grinding acorns gathered from the surrounding oaks. The Sequoia-Kings Canyon area has many such sites, probably locations of summer camps used regularly for many years by groups seeking relief from the hot temperatures of the foothills.

Just past the mortars, the trail forks again, and again we bear to the left, descending gently and returning to the start of the Huckleberry Meadow loop at 3.1 miles. Turn right at this trail junction and continue back the way you came, reaching the trailhead and parking area at 4 miles.   ■

Moro Rock

Hike #14: Log Meadow

Distance	6 miles
Level of difficulty	Easy
Child rating	10 years and up
Starting elevation	6880 feet
Highest point on trail	7280 feet
Topographic maps	Giant Forest, Lodgepole 7.5';
	Giant Forest, Triple Divide Peak 15'
Guidebook map	6

In the paved, fenced and easily reached Giant Forest area of Sequoia National Park, the majestic big trees are like creatures in a zoo, penned in and gawked at by camera-wielding hordes of spectators. But with very little effort, a hiker can leave the crowds behind and enjoy the sight of the huge trees in their natural surroundings.

This loop hike offers just such an opportunity. It starts at the General Sherman tree, which, at a height of 275 feet and an estimated weight of 2.8 million pounds, is the planet's largest living thing. Parking, restrooms and water are available nearby in a large lot off Generals Highway about 2 miles north of Giant Forest Village.

From the foot of the Sherman Tree, follow the paved Congress Trail to the right, along the edge of the roadway and then downhill into a small ravine. At 0.5 mile, the trail forks, the right branch being a cutoff that lets you return to the parking lot along the Congress Trail loop. Ignoring the cutoff and continuing ahead, we reach a junction with the Alta Trail at 0.7 mile.

Past the junction, following the signs for the Trail of the Sequoias, the trail begins to climb and passes the Chief Sequoyah Tree, one of the huge specimens that gave Giant Forest its name. At 1 mile, the trail enters an area that was burned deliberately as part of a Park Service program of controlled fires begun in 1979. The program's goal is to recreate the conditions thought to have existed in the 19th century, before the forest's human overseers began putting out naturally occurring fires in a misguided effort to protect the big trees.

At 1.4 miles the trail levels and soon passes out of the burn area. The transition is notable, and even a child will notice how the unburned area, the result of a century of fire suppression, is so choked with debris as to make germination of trees or other plants unlikely.

At 2 miles the trail passes a pair of magnificent towering sequoias, crosses small Crescent Creek and then curves south, maintaining a level course. At 3 miles, it reaches another junction. One-half mile ahead lies the High Sierra Trail, which leads nearly 63 miles from Crescent Meadow across the heart of the Sierra

Nevada all the way to the summit of Mt. Whitney. We, however, leave that challenge for another day and bear to the right, dropping steeply at times to the edge of Log Meadow. At the edge of the meadow, the trail forks again, and again we bear to the right, reaching Tharps Log at 3.3 miles.

The log was the summer home of Hale Tharp, who came to the area in 1856 and established a cattle ranch along the Kaweah River where it leaves the Sierra. In summer Tharp drove his cattle into the mountains to graze in the meadows, and he was among the first white men to live in the Giant Forest area. Inside the fire-hollowed sequoia that served as his mountain cabin are rough-hewn benches, a bed, a table, and a stone fireplace. Planks form a door and a window, and enclose a small entryway.

The log is in a small clearing at the edge of the meadow, and benches scattered around it make this a fine, restful place for a lunch break. The trail forks here, and our path lies to the right

Past the log, the trail climbs a bit and then descends to the Chimney Tree, a hollow snag that was burned more than 60 years ago by a careless camper. Just beyond, the trail forks three more times in quick succession, each left branch heading toward the Crescent Meadow parking lot. Each time our route lies to the right, as the trail makes a moderate ascent of the low ridge we crossed earlier.

At 4.4 miles the trail again branches, the left fork leading along the Huckleberry Meadow Trail back to Giant Forest Village. We continue to the right toward Circle Meadow. Another 200 yards bring us to yet another fork, but this time we bear left, cross narrow Circle Meadow and then pass through a fire-scarred tree called Black Arch. A few yards farther the trail leads between the Pillars of Hercules, two ravaged sequoias bracketing the path that were apparently named after park officials had run out of presidents and generals to honor.

The trail leads to another junction, and again we bear right, reaching Cattle Cabin at 5 miles. The restored log structure dates to the early 1900s and was used by cattlemen who supplied the nearby lodges with meat and milk, using Circle Meadow for a slaughtering pen.

Passing the Founders Group, the Room Tree and the McKinley Tree, the trail continues straight and leads us the remaining mile back to the General Sherman Tree. ■

Tharp's Log with improvements

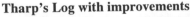

Hike #15: Mehrten Meadow

Distance	8 miles
Level of difficulty	Strenuous
Child rating	10 and up
Starting elevation	7270 feet
Highest point on trail	9040 feet
Topographic maps	Lodgepole 7.5';
	Triple Divide Peak 15'
Guidebook map	7

Spectacular views of the Great Western Divide await hikers who follow this trail to Panther Gap and Mehrten Meadow. The divide, often mistaken by early explorers for the real Sierra Crest—which parallels it but lies about 15 miles east of it—towers thousands of feet above the canyons of the Middle Fork Kaweah River and its tributaries. The divide is a string of gleaming, jagged peaks that are snowbound even in midsummer.

The trail begins at the Wolverton parking area and for the first 1.8 miles follows the route of hike #12, the Heather Lake trail. At the junction, however, bear to the right, toward Panther Gap.

Past the junction the trail leads over an open hillside covered with ferns, crossing a series of small streams that water the lush vegetation of Panther Meadow and join to form Wolverton Creek. At 2.1 miles the climb abruptly steepens, crossing an open, brush-covered slope dotted with occasional trees, many of them broken off 10 or more feet from the ground. At times zigzagging up the steep slope, the trail reaches Panther Gap at 2.8 miles.

The gap, a low point on the ridge above the canyon of the Middle Fork Kaweah River, provides magnificent views. The river winds 4400 feet below, a tiny, shimmering ribbon flowing between sere, brown slopes dotted with rock outcroppings. To the southeast, the jagged peaks of the Great Western Divide thrust upward, reaching elevations of more than 12,000 feet—more than a mile and a half above the river at your feet.

The trail forks here, and our path leads to the left. If you have children with you on this hike, or if you are afraid of heights, you may wish to turn back from this point. For beyond Panther Gap, the trail leads east across the face of the steep, rocky ridge, crossing a number of avalanche chutes that plummet steeply, thousands of feet to the valley below. The narrow trail is open and rocky, and there is little between the hiker and the precipitous drop but an occasional tree or bush.

Beyond the steep slope the trail forks again, and again we bear to the left, leaving the open, rocky slope and entering forest cover. Then the trail turns north briefly, climbing a bit and reaching Mehrten Meadow at 4 miles.

The meadow, named after a pioneer ranching family that used the area in the late 1800s, is a delightful gem, well-watered and brimming with wildflowers. Several campsites are located here on the banks of a small stream, and the restful music of falling water forms a soothing background as you contemplate the view.

Return the way you came.   ■

Cascade on Sheep Creek

Hike #16: Muir Grove

Distance	4 miles
Level of difficulty	Moderate
Child rating	5 and up
Starting elevation	6750 feet
Highest point on trail	6830 feet
Topographic maps	Muir Grove 7.5'; Giant Forest 15'
Guidebook map	8

This fairly easy trail leads out of recently renovated Dorst Creek campground to a fine stand of sequoias along the edge of Pine Ridge. At one time, judging by the markings on old maps, the trail extended beyond the grove, encircling Pine Ridge and passing through other stands of sequoias. It appears, however, that disuse and lack of maintenance have allowed it to slide into oblivion beyond Muir Grove.

Dorst Campground is named after Capt. Joseph Dorst, commander of the troop of cavalry assigned to protect newly created Sequoia and General Grant national parks in 1891. In those days before the creation of the National Park Service, protection and governance of the parks fell to the military, which each spring sent a detachment of troops from the Presidio in San Francisco to establish camp and spend the summer evicting sheep and cattle herders, miners, hunters and loggers from the new federal preserves. Not until 1914 was the Army relieved of this task, for which it was ill-suited, and civilian management of the parks instituted.

The trailhead is about 50 yards past the entrance to the group camping area, at a log bridge on the right side of the main road through the campground. Restrooms and water are nearby.

The broad, dusty trail descends gently through dense forest dominated by white fir. At 0.1 mile the trail forks, the right branch leading toward Generals Highway and the left, our path, leading along the edge of a small, flower-strewn meadow fed by an unnamed tributary of Dorst Creek.

At 0.8 mile the trail begins a moderate climb, zigzagging up the ridge and emerging at 1 mile on a rocky, bare promontory that offers views west across a steep ravine. Atop the ridge on the other side, the dome-shaped crowns of Muir Grove's sequoias are visible, easy to pick out from the surrounding forest because of their distinctive shape and color.

The trail then descends part way into the ravine, working southwest along a more open hillside dotted with wildflowers and an occasional oak tree. At 1.5 miles the trail nears the stream that splashes along the bottom of the ravine, and the sun-loving, drought-tolerant plants give way to lush ferns and grasses. After crossing this rivulet, the trail doubles back along the west slope and then climbs gently to the top of the ridge, arriving at the grove at 2 miles.

The trees stand on a sunny hillside carpeted by lupine, the ruddy sequoia bark glowing when the low-angle morning light strikes it. Although near the campground—which, with 218 sites, is the second-largest in Sequoia-Kings Canyon national parks—Muir Grove receives only a small fraction of the number of visitors who descend on the better-known sequoia groups near the park highways. As a result, hikers will most likely be free to wander in silence, alone with the trees, undisturbed by traffic noise or jostling sightseers armed with camcorders.

A bear-chewed sign, all but illegible, points toward additional features along the trail, which appears to continue beyond the grove. It does, forking just past the main group of trees. But after a short distance both tracks disappear without leading to anything as captivating as the grove itself, which is a pleasant spot for a picnic.

Return the way you came.   ■

Hike #17: Tokopah Falls

Distance	3.5 miles
Level of difficulty	Easy
Child rating	5 years and up
Starting elevation	6720 feet
Highest point on trail	7250 feet
Topographic maps	Lodgepole 7.5';
	Triple Divide Peak 15'
Guidebook map	7

Lodgepole Campground, center of most activities in Sequoia National Park, sits in the bottom of the deep, glacially carved canyon of the Kaweah River's Marble Fork. As a result, nearly all the trails originating here climb steeply to reach the surrounding high country, presenting much difficulty to casual hikers and those accompanied by youngsters.

The Tokopah Trail is an exception. Paralleling the boulder-filled bed of the Marble Fork, it climbs gently through a thick forest of incense-cedar, Jeffrey pine and Douglas-fir. Accompanied by the music of falling water, you may see some of the abundant bird and animal life—deer, marmots, several varieties of squirrels and chipmunks—that lives in the valley. And at the end of the easy trail, the shade of the trees is left behind as the forest drops away and the sheer, naked granite cliffs walling in the Tokopah Valley rear more than 1000 feet into the air. Down this rocky face cascades Tokopah Falls, a sight best viewed early in the season when the water is high.

The trail begins at the right side of the road, just over the bridge in the middle of the campground. A large parking area, restrooms and water are nearby. Heading northeast, the trail follows the riverbank, wandering away at times to climb over granite outcrops but always remaining within sight of the rocky streambed. From time to time, the trail passes relatively open, grassy areas that are filled with bursts of wildflower color in season.

The valley's flat floor is evidence that a glacier helped carve it, since canyons cut by rivers alone generally have a V-shaped cross section. Indeed, during the series of Sierran glacial advances, which began about 2.5 million years ago and ended a scant 10,000 years ago—practically yesterday in the scale of geologic time—this canyon floor was buried 500 feet deep by a moving river of ice.

The glacier, like those that carved most of the high canyons and valleys of this part of the Sierra, ground away at the sides and bottom of the Marble Fork canyon, widening and flattening the canyon floor. At 0.9 mile you can see one of the products of all that icy excavation: Directly on the other side of the river stands the Watchtower, a sheer face of granite that juts from the canyon wall and soars

1600 feet above the river. Too tough to be ground away by the glacier, the Watchtower was left behind after the ice plucked away the surrounding rock.

At 1.5 miles the trail leaves the forest cover and emerges into a world of stone, clothed by sun-loving plants such as oak, blue elderberry and manzanita. The climb steepens, and the path becomes rocky, climbing over and winding between huge chunks of granite that have tumbled from the high cliffs that wall in the end of the valley. A child may balk at this point, and if so, your choices are to halt at the edge of the forest and view the waterfall from afar, or carry the child over the rough spots.

At just over 1.7 miles the trail ends on a level, boulder-rimmed bench at the base of the cliffs. Not far away, the river cascades down the polished stone. Signs warn against proceeding beyond the trail's end, because of the danger posed by the slippery, unstable rock slope. Park literature notes ominously that several hikers have been killed in this area.

The flat, sunny trail terminus provides a nice view of the spectacular surrounding scenery and a comfortable place for a snack. With all that, who needs to go looking for thrills?

Return the way you came.   ■

Trails of Grant Grove

Grant Grove is the oldest section of Kings Canyon National Park, having been set aside as General Grant National Park in 1890 by the same federal law that established Yosemite National Park. Included in its attractions is the famous General Grant tree, third-largest sequoia in the world, as well as other sequoia groves and ridgetop views that on clear days reach from the Great Western Divide on the east to the Coast Ranges on the west.

Grant Grove lies north of the Big Stump park entrance, on Highway 180 just north of its junction with Generals Highway. Campgrounds and full visitor services are available. See the chapter "Facilities" for details. Redwood Mountain, which is included in this section because it shares the same general characteristics as Grant Grove and lies only 6.5 miles from the Grant Grove Visitor Center, is to the east along Generals Highway. ■

In Grant Grove

Ron Felzer

Hike #18: Big Stump Basin

Distance	1 mile
Level of difficulty	Easy
Child rating	3 years and up
Starting elevation	6200 feet
Highest point on trail	6400 feet
Topographic maps	General Grant Grove 7.5';
	Giant Forest 15'
Guidebook map	9

Any visit to giant sequoia territory should include a side trip to Big Stump Basin. Nothing drives home more forcefully the need for legislative protection of the groves than a look at how, despite inadequate technology and lack of transportation, loggers in the late 1800s began chopping their way through the big trees.

The Big Stump Trail begins at a parking area inside Kings Canyon National Park just beyond the Big Stump Entrance Station. The path, paved at first, starts next to a coin-operated vending machine where you can buy a leaflet describing some of the features you will encounter. Nearby are several picnic tables, unattractively located in the treeless parking lot itself, and a restroom facility with running water.

The trail heads downhill into the basin, passing through manzanita and a second-growth forest of young incense-cedar, Jeffrey pine, sugar pine and Douglas-fir. The progenitors of these trees were felled, along with the basin's sequoias, starting in 1883, when the Smith Comstock mill was built here.

Immediately the trail passes the Resurrection Tree, an old sequoia that continues to flourish despite having had its top blasted and left scarred by lightning. As the path continues gently downhill, it passes what's been dubbed the Shake Pile, remnants of a sequoia that, like all the big trees felled by loggers, was split into shakes and fence posts. Because the trees are so massive, and because their wood is brittle and short-grained, they tend to shatter when felled, making them unsuitable for board lumber. Instead, using wedges and mallets, the loggers split off what usable pieces they could, leaving the rest of the tree to rot.

The trail then forks. To the right it leads to the Shattered Giant, a tree that was cut down in a way contrary to the prevailing wisdom of the day, which recommended dropping trees uphill to minimize the impact. When it fell, downhill and across a streambed, it exploded into useless fragments. To the left, the fork our route follows, the trail passes the Burnt Monarch, a charred snag, and about 50 yards farther on reaches a pair of beautiful young sequoias planted in 1888 by a lumberjack who lived in the area. They're worth examining to get an idea of the pace at which the giant trees grow.

The trail, level now, reaches the edge of the meadow and passes the site of the former Comstock Mill. All that remains is a rectangular pattern of timbers jutting from the ground. Around the meadow's edges are ghostly gray stumps protruding from the undergrowth, and in its center are piles of sawdust, still pink and fresh-looking after more than 100 years.

At another fork, the trail leads left to a "feather bed," a long trench that loggers dug and filled with branches in an effort to cushion the fall when they cut down a big tree. Now choked with willows and other growth, it looks more like a creekbed than a man-made feature, but if you look carefully you can see pieces of a tree still in place where it dropped. Other feather beds can be seen throughout the area by those with careful eyes.

Bearing left at the next trail fork brings us to the Mark Twain Stump, where a display tells the story of this massive forest monarch, felled in 1891 so that sections could be sent to museums for display. A staircase leads to the top of the stump, and children will probably enjoy trying to count the rings while scrambling around on the flat surface.

The trail then climbs, crossing the park highway and traversing the side of a ridge above it as it leads north. In about 200 yards a spur leads to the Sawed Tree, opposite a thick grove of arrow-straight young sequoias growing in the clearing left when their giant parents were chopped down. Partly cut through but not toppled, the Sawed Tree appears perfectly healthy and has healed most of the scars left by the loggers, demonstrating the amazing resilience of the species.

As the trail turns west and continues back to the parking lot, it allows glimpses of the park road, where loaded logging trucks still rumble down the grade, carrying timber cut in nearby Sequoia National Forest. The Forest Service, unlike the Park Service, encourages logging under its official policy of multiple use.

After passing under the park road through a culvert, the trail forks, the left branch returning to the parking area and the right leading to Hitchcock Meadow and beyond. ■

Hike #19: North Grove Loop

Distance	1.5 miles
Level of difficulty	Easy
Child rating	5 and up
Starting elevation	6350 feet
Lowest point on trail	6000 feet
Topographic maps	General Grant Grove, Hume 7.5';
	Giant Forest, Tehipite Dome 15'
Guidebook map	10

Old topographic maps show this route as an unpaved road, which it once was. Now, however, it is closed to vehicles, and the broad, graded surface makes for an easy hike through a lovely sun-dappled forest of sequoia, sugar pine, white fir and dogwood. Although the trail is near one of the most popular attractions in Kings Canyon National Park—the General Grant Tree—the hiker soon leaves behind the cacophony of the crowds and enters a realm of solitude.

The trail begins at the lower end of the Grant Tree parking area, past the gate at the northwest side of the lot reserved for tour buses and recreational vehicles. Follow the paved road downhill just over 0.1 mile, and then bear right where the sign indicates the start of the North Grove Loop Trail.

The trail continues downhill, through a forest of cedar, sugar pine and an occasional sequoia. As it winds along, the road stays close to a trickle of water that feeds meadow flowers and grasses, and accounts for the presence of so many moisture-dependent sequoias.

The trail bottoms out and turns west at about 0.7 mile, soon reaching an overgrown track leading into the forest to the right. A sign identifies it as the old Millwood Road, which formerly led to a logging town that sent timber by flume to the valley town of Sanger in the 1890s.

On the left side of the road at the Millwood junction is a giant sequoia that appears to have been killed by fire, an extremely rare occurrence. The trees' thick bark makes them resistant to flames, and in fact they rely on periodic fires to clear the undergrowth and allow their seeds to germinate.

From here the road turns south and then curves east, climbing steadily and joining the road to Sequoia Lake at 1.2 miles. Stay to your left here, and follow the road uphill back to the Grant Tree parking area.   ■

Hike #20: Park Ridge

Distance	5.2 miles
Level of difficulty	Moderate
Child rating	5 and up
Starting elevation	7300 feet
Highest point on trail	7720 feet
Topographic maps	General Grant Grove, Hume 7.5'; Giant Forest, Tehipite Dome 15'
Guidebook map	11

This trail follows the crest of the ridge that marks the east border of the former General Grant National Park, and provides expansive views of the Sierra foothills and the San Joaquin Valley to the west, the peaks of the Monarch Divide to the northeast, and the Great Western Divide to the southeast. As a bonus, it ends at one of the few mountain fire lookouts still in use in California. (Most have been shut down and replaced by more cost-effective fire spotting methods such as aerial and satellite surveillance.)

To reach the trailhead, you must drive a narrow, steep, paved but decrepit road 2.5 miles from the Grant Grove visitor center to the Panoramic Point parking area. Recreational vehicles and trailers are prohibited. Restrooms and picnic tables are provided at the parking area, but there is no water.

The trail leaves from the northeast end of the parking area and climbs immediately along a paved course to Panoramic Point. From here, on a clear day, the view to the northeast discloses the wild backcountry of Kings Canyon National Park. After about 300 yards the trail returns to dirt, levels out and follows the open, rocky ridgetop. To the right, views of the San Joaquin Valley appear through the manzanita and other tough members of the chaparral plant community. On the rare clear day, when the usual smog and haze of the Central Valley have been blown away by a storm, the shadowy outline of the Coast Ranges—more than 100 miles distant—may been seen.

The trail passes into forest at 0.7 mile and begins a moderate climb, leveling off at about 1 mile. It then descends, alternating between forest and open, sunny areas and reaching a dirt fire road at 1.5 miles. Bear left, following the road for about 50 yards. Keep an eye out to your right for the sign indicating the Azalea Trail, about 50 feet from the side of the road. Head for the sign and turn left, bearing southeast, at the junction it marks.

The trail climbs a bit, levels and then descends to rejoin the fire road at 2.4 miles. Turn right and follow the road another 0.2 mile to the fire lookout, which crouches on the edge of the ridge.

A fire spotter lives here during the summer months, keeping an eye out for the telltale wisps of smoke that might signal the start of a potentially disastrous forest fire. Do not ascend the tower without first asking permission from the person on duty—who is usually more than happy to grant it. From the tower itself the view is quite spectacular, reaching from the Great Valley in the west to the Great Western Divide in the east.

From the tower, return back along the fire road and remain on it when you reach the trail. The road leads along the east park boundary, crossing briefly into adjoining Sequoia National Forest. This segment of the hike is instructive, for as soon as you cross the boundary you enter a landscape that has been logged and used as a livestock range. The trampled, churned soil, deprived of forest cover and then stripped by cattle, presents a stark contrast to the shaded, thick growth in the national park, where grazing and logging are prohibited. The precise demarcation can be seen on the hillside to the southeast, where the park border is visible as a straight line formed by the meeting point between forest and clearcut.

The mostly level road re-enters the national park at 3.5 miles. Continue along it another 1.6 miles to the paved road that leads to the Panoramic Point parking area, and proceed up the paved road 0.1 mile to your car.   ■

**Fire lookout
on Park Ridge**

Hike #21: Redwood Canyon

Distance	6.5 miles
Level of difficulty	Moderate
Child rating	10 years and up
Starting elevation	6200 feet
Highest point on trail	6400 feet
Topographic maps	General Grant Grove 7.5'; Giant Forest 15'
Guidebook map	12

Although it is only about 6 miles from the heavily visited Grant Grove area, this part of Kings Canyon National Park is lightly used. This loop hike offers a chance to explore the Redwood Mountain sequoia grove, the world's largest, in solitude, and can easily be walked in half a day; allow a full day if you are accompanied by youngsters.

The trailhead is at Redwood Saddle, which is reached by a dirt road that branches south from Generals Highway at Quail Flat, 4 miles east of the Big Stump entrance. The road, while very narrow and winding, is suitable for passenger cars with good clearance but is not advised for motor homes, trailers or overloaded station wagons.

After 1.5 miles the road splits, the left fork leading to a parking area. Our trail leaves from the northeast side of the lot, next to a sign "Hart Tree." No water or restrooms are available at the trailhead.

The trail descends immediately into a small ravine filled with a stand of giant sequoias, winding close enough to the big trees for kids to run their hands over the soft, furry bark, and reaching a junction at 0.3 mile. Bear to the left, following the sign that directs you to the redwood log cabin, Hart Tree, Fallen Goliath and Redwood Creek.

At 0.5 mile the trail crosses a creek, a trickle lined with ferns, grasses and lupine, and then curves around the far side of the ravine and climbs slightly. At 0.8 mile it reaches the Redwood Log Cabin, which is built not from logs, as one might expect, but from *a* log—a downed and partly fire-hollowed sequoia, to be exact. Rough planks were used to cover some holes in the log, and stone fireplaces were built at both ends. This rude dwelling probably dates from the late 1800s, when the area was acquired by those interested in its logging potential.

For the next mile, the trail ascends the east side of Redwood Canyon, the climb ranging from gentle to moderate. Through the trees the hiker catches glimpses of Redwood Mountain on the other side of the canyon. At 1.9 miles the trail reaches an exposed outcropping of granite that provides expansive views of the surrounding terrain and offers a pleasant spot for a breather. Away to the southeast, Big

Baldy rears its head, a prominent outcropping of naked stone nearly 3,000 feet above the canyon floor.

At 2.1 miles the trail reaches Hart Meadow. Above the meadow to the northeast is Buena Vista Peak. After crossing Buena Vista Creek, which drains the meadow, the trail begins gently descending, passing through magnificent stands of the big trees and reaching the tunnel log at 2.7 miles. The trail passes right through the hollowed log, providing a treat for young hikers and forcing their elders to duck.

After crossing the small East Fork Redwood Creek, the trail climbs and at 3 miles reaches a steep spur branching to the left that leads to the Hart Tree. The huge, gnarled, fire-scarred giant is named after William Hart, a sawmill operator who acquired 80 acres in this area in 1888. The main trail continues to the right, crossing an unnamed creek that cascades down a slick stone chute through a fern-lined grotto.

At 4.5 miles, the trail forks. Bear right, past the Fallen Goliath—an enormous downed tree—and walk gently downhill to a crossing of Redwood Creek, mostly dry by late season. The trail crosses the rocky creekbed and at 5 miles reaches a fork. From here a trail continues downstream toward mining prospects at the entrance to the canyon. Turning right, we begin the return trip to the parking lot, following the course of the creek upstream.

Our route here follows an old roadbed, identified on the 15' topographic map as a Jeep Trail. The route itself is probably that of a wagon road built either by loggers, who fed a mill on Redwood Mountain that managed to cut 2 million board feet of lumber as early as 1874, or prospectors, who found noncommercial quantities of several minerals in the canyon.

A few yards farther, the trail reaches a junction with the Sugarbowl Trail, which leads up the side of Redwood Mountain and eventually back to the parking lot. Our route takes the more direct path up the canyon, ascending moderately past an awe-inspiring stand of eight giant sequoias, standing in isolated splendor along the stream bank.

At 5.8 miles a faint track leads to the right. Following it for about 50 yards takes you to a downed sequoia that has been partly cut up. Probably the site of one of the shake camps sprinkled throughout the area, where fallen trees were salvaged early in the century for such things as fence posts and roofing shakes, the log shows clear saw marks, and squared-off fragments litter the area.

Another 200 yards brings you to a sign that reads "Research Area, Ecology of Sequoia, Do not Disturb." The area was the site of controlled experimental burns set in the mid-1960s by Park Service biologists to test the effect of fire on forest growth and sequoia regeneration. The experiments showed that without occasional hot-burning fires to clear the understory and associated debris, the giant trees do not reproduce.

From here, the trail continues its climb back up Redwood Canyon, reaching the first junction of the hike and following the left fork back to the parking area. ■

Trails of Mineral King

Mineral King Valley was the focus of one of the epic legal battles in the long fight to preserve the great scenic areas of the Sierra Nevada.

Despite its name, Mineral King never made anyone rich. The traces of silver ore discovered in the late 1800s drew hundreds of hopeful miners to this high, rugged valley, and they cut its trees for firewood and mine timbers, tunneled into the colorful rock of its barren peaks, trampled its plant life, and cut roads and trails across its slopes. But they never found commercially valuable deposits. Bankruptcy drove away those who hadn't already been discouraged by winter avalanches.

In 1965 Mineral King drew the attention of a different sort of fortune-hunter. Responding to a request from the Forest Service, which was managing the valley as a federal game preserve, the Walt Disney Corp. proposed a $35 million ski resort in Mineral King including as many as 27 chair lifts. Hotels, gas stations, restaurants, parking garages and assorted other structures would fill the valley, which would be reached by a new $30 million highway that the state had agreed to build though a part of Sequoia National Park.

The Sierra Club, after being rebuffed in repeated efforts to halt the project through administrative channels, in 1969 sued in federal court to block it. The case eventually wound up before the U.S. Supreme Court, which ruled that the Sierra Club did not have legal standing to sue the government on behalf of a game preserve. But in so doing, the court broadly hinted that the club could try again, by showing how its members would be harmed by Disney's proposed project. The club did so in 1972, and also added new claims under the new Environmental Policy Act. This time it was successful, and the court ordered the government to complete an environmental impact report on the ski-resort plan.

As a result, thousands of people and dozens of public and private agencies were given the opportunity to comment on the project. Most were against it, citing its effects on wildlife and on the integrity of nearby Sequoia National Park. Enthusiasm for the project waned at Disney, and the state withdrew its offer to build the road. By 1977 the project had been abandoned, and in 1978 Mineral King Valley was added to the park. ∎

Hike #22: Cold Springs Nature Trail

Distance	1 mile
Level of difficulty	Easy
Child rating	3 and up
Starting elevation	7500 feet
Highest point on trail	7550 feet
Topographic maps	Mineral King 7.5'; Mineral King 15'
Guidebook map	13

It is not easy to reach Mineral King Valley; visitors must endure 25 miles of primitive, twisting, climbing road suited more to horse-drawn wagons than to modern automobiles. And even when you've arrived, the valley seems intent on keeping its scenic mysteries hidden, with formidable barriers of altitude and topography.

To really appreciate this remote region of Sequoia National Park, you must be willing to climb out of the pleasant, steep-walled valley into the rocky basins on its rim, places of rugged grandeur swept by cold winds and wreathed on many days in a swirling mist. The climbs are steep, begin at an already considerable elevation of at least 7,500 feet, and often lead into the treeless alpine zone above 10,000 feet. It is not a place the gives up its treasures to the casual visitor. It takes time, time to grow acclimated to the thin air, time to explore.

The Cold Springs Nature Trail is a good place to start. It is best to spend a couple of days in the valley before attempting any of the longer hikes, and in that time you can roam the valley floor and follow this self-guiding path, which offers a good introduction to the ecology and the plant life of the area.

The level trail begins next to campsite #6 in Cold Springs Campground. It passes through a grassy area dotted with cottonwoods and aspens, and filled with a rainbow profusion of wildflowers. Signs along the way identify some of the characteristic flora of this life zone.

After about ¼ mile the signed nature trail loops back along the bank of the North Fork Kaweah River. If you continue past the loop for a short distance, you enter a field of even more extravagant flowers, and then climb a bit to the edge of the red fir forest that blankets those slopes which haven't been cleared by the periodic avalanches that roar through the valley in winter.

The trail fades out in a marshy grassland about ½ mile from the campground. At this point, turn around and take the other side of the loop to return to the trailhead.   ■

Hike #23: Crystal Lake

Distance	10 miles
Level of difficulty	Strenuous
Child rating	Not recommended for children
Starting elevation	7760 feet
Highest point on trail	10750 feet
Topographic maps	Mineral King 7.5'; Mineral King 15'
Guidebook map	14

Many of the trails in Mineral King follow the routes established by miners in the 1870s, when the valley underwent a brief and ultimately fruitless silver boom. The mines that still dot the surrounding hillsides never produced commercially valuable ore, but the miners left their mark in the form of gaping shafts, abandoned equipment, piles of rubble and myriad footpaths crisscrossing the slopes.

The trail to Crystal Lake follows one such route, distinguished by its tendency to follow the shortest distance between two points—even if it means climbing straight up a precipitous slope. As a result, hikers should undertake this steep, rocky trip only if they're wearing sturdy shoes and aren't afraid of a rigorous climb at high elevation.

The reward is magnificent views and the barren, rocky scenery of a seldom-visited alpine lake basin.

The trail begins at the Monarch Lakes-Sawtooth Pass trailhead, a mile east of the ranger station on the Mineral King Road. Yellow-bellied marmots, also known as whistle pigs or, erroneously, groundhogs (they are relatives of the true groundhog), make their homes beneath the logs and boulders here, and have been known to gnaw on the electrical wiring, radiator hoses and fan belts of parked cars. No one has offered a satisfactory explanation for this behavior, nor is there a sure method of preventing the damage. About all you can do is park well away from their dens, open your hood and hope for the best. Since the nearest automotive service is over an hour away, and the ranger station stocks no spare parts, it is prudent when visiting Mineral King to carry backup belts and hoses.

The rocky trail leaves the north side of the parking area and climbs steeply up an open hillside of sage and manzanita, switchbacking several times. At 0.5 mile it divides, the left fork leading to Timber Gap. Bear right, climbing moderately past stands of Sierra juniper up the Monarch Creek drainage. At 1 mile, the trail reaches Groundhog Meadow, where your arrival will more than likely be announced by the characteristic high-pitched whistle of a marmot. The small meadow lies in a bowl surrounded by ragged cliffs, and is filled with wildflowers in early summer. The trail forks again here, and our route goes to the right, across the creek.

The trail enters dense forest of red and white fir as it begins switchbacking up the moist, spring-watered slope. Along the way it passes colorful outcroppings of ice-polished metamorphic rock. The trail then rounds a corner and heads southeast into Chihuahua Bowl, named after a famous mining region in Mexico, at 3 miles. The climb continues, and expansive views begin to unfold.

Another ½ mile brings you to a trail junction. The left fork leads 1.2 miles to Monarch Lake, while our faint path lies to the right, climbing with little regard for topography up the rocky slope toward a low saddle.

At 4 miles and 10,400 feet elevation, the trail passes the remnants of the Chihuahua Mine, off to the right at the top of the ridge. The trail then contours along the side of the ridge, clinging precariously to the unstable rock. Below lie the tiny Cobalt Lakes, perched on benches above cascading Crystal Creek, which can be reached by a steep spur trail.

The trail to Crystal Lake continues across a treacherous slope, over rocks ranging in size from eggs to footballs. It requires concentration to keep from losing your footing, and frequent stops to catch your breath. The faint path switchbacks up the wall and then levels off in the final hundred yards to arrive at the outlet of the lake at 5 miles. It was a naturally formed glacial tarn, a small body of meltwater left in a cirque where a glacier was born, but it was dammed by the Mt. Whitney Power Company near the turn of the century to raise its level in order to supply more water to the East Fork Kaweah River in summer.

Views from the barren shore of the lake, ice-covered until midsummer, are spectacular. To the south is Rainbow Mountain, which, like Mineral Peak to the north, displays the colorful meeting of the dark metamorphic rocks and the lighter, much younger granites that welled up beneath them when the range was forming. To the southwest, across the upper end of Mineral King Valley, are White Chief Peak, Eagle Crest and other rocky pinnacles, many of them protecting their own unseen lakes.

Return the way you came.   ■

Peaks above the Crystal Lake Trail

Hike #24: Eagle Lake

Distance	6.8 miles
Level of difficulty	Strenuous
Child rating	10 and up
Starting elevation	7830 feet
Highest point on trail	10010 feet
Topographic maps	Mineral King 7.5'; Mineral King 15'
Guidebook map	15

The trail to Eagle Lake begins at the Eagle Crest parking area, 1.5 miles east of the ranger station on the Mineral King road, near a collection of privately owned summer cabins. Be sure not to block any of the driveways when you park.

Following a gentle grade, the trail proceeds south, paralleling the course of the East Fork Kaweah River. The hillsides here are clothed in sage, while the meadow below wears a thick coat of grass and wildflowers. Across the valley lie the corrals and outbuildings of the Mineral King Pack Station, which runs horse trips into the backcountry.

Several hundred yards up the valley the trail crosses small Spring Creek on a wooden bridge. The creek is one of Mineral King's mysteries, gushing from the mountainside several hundred feet above the trail. Its source is unknown, but the presence of a porous layer of marble above the spring makes it likely that the creek begins life elsewhere on the mountainside and travels through subterranean caves to the spring.

At 0.8 mile the trail crosses Eagle Creek, and then forks at 1 mile. The left branch leads to White Chief Canyon; our route is to the right. A series of switchbacks leads us through thicker stands of white fir, across wildflower-strewn hillsides and onto a gentle slope near the dry bed of Eagle Creek.

At 1.5 miles the explanation for the absence of water in Eagle Creek becomes clear, as the trail leads past a large sinkhole that swallows the entire stream. A second sinkhole is visible if you follow the dry streambed downhill a short distance, indicating that the ground beneath the trail is honeycombed with water-carved passages. One theory is that part of Eagle Creek—which reappears below us on the mountainside—is diverted amid those hidden passages and emerges as Spring Creek.

The trail, more level now, passes through a thick forest. At 1.8 miles it splits again, and we take the left fork along the bank of the creek, which passes through small meadows frequented by mule deer. The route then climbs, moderately at first and then more steeply. At 3.1 miles it begins working its way across the talus at the base of a granite ridge. The rock here shows many darker inclusions, remnants of the older rock incompletely absorbed by the molten granite when it welled up from deep in the earth more than 100 million years ago.

At 3.2 miles the trail reaches the outlet of Eagle Lake, which like many other small lakes in the area has been dammed to increase its storage capacity. The trail continues nearly to the end of the lake; midway a rocky promontory juts into the mirrorlike water and offers a scenic resting spot.

This is a popular backpacking destination, and a primitive, partly enclosed pit toilet has been set up to the right of the trail to minimize human pollution.

Above the lake rises the jagged edge of Eagle Crest, and views to the northeast include glimpses of the snow-capped peaks of the Great Western Divide. The picturesque, gnarled trunks of foxtail pine, a lover of high elevations, frame the scene.

Return the way you came.   ■

Foxtail pine and peaks above Mineral King Valley

Hike #25: Lower Mosquito Lake

Distance	6.5 miles
Level of difficulty	Moderate
Child rating	10 and up
Starting elevation	7830 feet
Highest point on trail	9300 feet
Topographic maps	Mineral King 7.5'; Mineral King 15'
Guidebook map	15

The Mosquito Lakes—there are five of them—perch in a small valley alongside Miner's Ridge overlooking the lower section of Mineral King Valley. Each is cupped in a rocky bowl, and together the bowls form a series of stair-steps leading downhill from the base of 11,127-foot Hengst Peak.

Such formations, known as glacial step lakes or paternoster lakes, after their resemblance to beads on a rosary, are common in terrain carved by glaciers. Each lake is dammed by a "riser" of rock that resisted the erosive power of the downhill-flowing glacier more than the softer or more jointed rock of the "tread." As a result the tread has been scooped out and the scoop collects runoff and meltwater, which form the characteristic lake.

Lower Mosquito Lake is the easiest to reach of all Mineral King's alpine lakes—if hiking anywhere at this elevation can be considered easy. The trail begins at the Eagle Crest parking area, and for the first 1.8 miles follows the same route as Hike #24.

At the trail junction 0.3 mile past the Eagle Creek sinkholes, however, take the right fork. The trail leads across level ground, crossing a small meadow rimmed by lodgepole pine, and then begins climbing along the side of Miner's Ridge through stands of red and white fir. At 2.3 miles the climb steepens and the trail makes a couple of switchbacks as it nears the top of the ridge, the highest point on the trail.

Crossing the ridgetop, the trail begins a somewhat steep descent through a dense forest of large firs. To the right, glimpses of Mineral King Valley and the mountains beyond are visible. The trail levels out somewhat at 2.7 miles, and the rushing sound of Mosquito Creek, which links the five lakes, can be heard.

At 3 miles, the trail reaches a boulder field at the edge of the small lake. The trail continues ¼ mile around the shore and then ends, but it is possible to scramble up the rocks and hike to the next lake. From there, more ambitious hikers can continue on and visit the other lakes in the chain, which sometimes reward anglers with catches of brook and rainbow trout.

Return the way you came.   ■

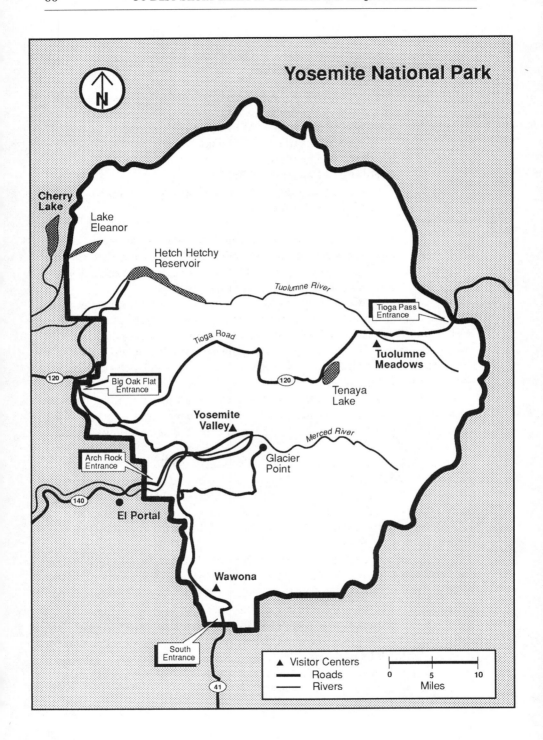

Yosemite National Park

Geological History

"No temple made with hands can compare with Yosemite," wrote John Muir, who is more strongly identified with the park than any of the hundreds of other writers, naturalists, scientists and explorers who have studied it.

> Every rock in its walls seems to glow with life. Some lean back in majestic repose; others, absolutely sheer or nearly so for thousands of feet, advance beyond their companions in thoughtful attitudes, giving welcome to storms and calms alike, seemingly aware, yet heedless, of everything going on about them. Awful in stern, immovable majesty, how softly these rocks are adorned, and how fine and reassuring the company they keep: their feet among beautiful groves and meadows, their brows in the sky. . . .

Though his language was more flowery than modern audiences are accustomed to, Muir expressed what everyone feels upon first visiting Yosemite. The valley and its surrounding peaks cast their spell over all who enter, conjuring through some peculiar alchemy of rock, light and falling water a unique aura. Other Sierran valleys are deeper, equally imposing granite peaks may be found elsewhere, the range is watered by hundreds of streams, each with its own beauty and charm. But nowhere is the sense of scenic harmony as great as in this "incomparable valley."

Yosemite National Park, located in the central Sierra Nevada, is more than just Yosemite Valley, although that is where most of its more than 3 million annual visitors spend most of their time. It protects within its 1,189 square miles some of the most famous and captivating scenery in the world—El Capitan, Half Dome, Bridalveil and Yosemite falls—but also hundreds of square miles of remoter backcountry, where the attraction of solitude is added to the grandeur of the landscape. As one of the world's best-known and most visited national parks, the features are so familiar, their images reproduced in so many books, on so many posters, calendars and postcards, that description here would serve little purpose. Instead, let us focus on how the landscape came to look the way it does.

The granite that forms the many domes, spires and cliff faces of Yosemite, both in the valley and the backcountry, was created starting about 250 million years ago (for a general description of the formation of the Sierra Nevada see the earlier chapter on Sequoia-Kings Canyon geology). Enormous masses of molten rock, called magma, welled upward from deep within the earth and intruded into the layers of older rocks close to the surface. Those plumes of magma then cooled and hardened in place, forming great bodies of granitic rock, still deep underground.

The process took as much as 150 million years, occurring in successive waves. About 60 million years ago, when Yosemite Valley was broad and shallow, a period of uplifting began. As the great block of the Sierra Nevada tilted and rose gradually above the surrounding terrain, erosion stripped away much of the overlying material and exposed some of the granite. The Merced River, which flows through the heart of Yosemite Valley, was initially a sluggish, meandering stream flanked by rolling hills and ridges 500-1,000 feet high. As the mountains rose and the gradient steepened, the Merced began to flow more forcefully, cutting more sharply into the valley floor.

When the uplifting began, Yosemite Valley had none of its famous waterfalls, for the tributary streams joined the Merced at its own level. But as the Merced cut farther into the floor of the valley the smaller side streams—which had far less erosive power because of their size—were unable to keep up. By about 3 million years ago some of the tributary streams reached the edge of the valley well above the level of the Merced River, and dropped to meet it in falls and cascades. Among them were Yosemite Creek, Ribbon Creek, Meadow Brook and Bridalveil Creek. Others, such as Indian, Illilouette and Tenaya creeks, had been able to keep up with the downward cutting Merced and joined it without cascade or falls.

Similar processes occurred throughout the Yosemite region as the Sierra tipped and rose, steepening the gradient of its streams and magnifying their erosive power. As the millenia passed, water, wind and other weathering agents carved away the thick beds of sedimentary rock laid down during ancient times when the region lay at the bottom of a shallow sea. Gradually the bare granite beneath was exposed to view, and the landscape took on a more rugged aspect.

The final stage in the evolution of the landscape we see today began with the first of several ice ages, starting about 2.5 million years ago. Average global temperatures dropped, allowing more snow to fall each winter than melted in the summer. The permanent snow fields expanded, a process that would later give birth to the great ice sheets that covered enormous expanses of North America and northern Europe. In the Sierra Nevada, alpine glaciers were born high among the peaks, often in basins protected from direct sunlight by surrounding cliffs. As they grew in size and weight, the glaciers began moving downhill, scraping away at the surrounding rock, ripping it up where it was fractured and least resistant, polishing it where it was hard and unjointed, quarrying the valleys with slow efficiency.

The first and greatest glacial advance filled Yosemite Valley to the brim with ice about 1 million years ago. Half Dome and El Capitan projected above the glacier, but most of the other features were swallowed—including Glacier Point, the popular spot from which millions of visitors have marveled at the panoramic view and the sheer drop thousands of feet to the valley below. Standing there today it is hard to imagine that the spot was once buried 500 feet beneath a glacier's surface.

At the same time, a far greater ice sheet blanketed Tuolumne Meadows, riding up and over such landmark features as Lembert Dome, and carved deeply into the Grand Canyon of the Tuolumne River. In total length the Tuolumne glacier reached 60 miles, making it one of the largest Sierran glaciers, extending 15 miles downstream from Hetch Hetchy Reservoir's O'Shaughnessy Dam.

Everywhere, the ice gouged and ripped at the landscape, using torn-off boulders and chunks of stone as carving tools. By the time the last of three waves of glaciation had receded from Yosemite Valley, the ice had broadened it to its present shape from the original **V** profile carved by the Merced, and had deepened it by about 2,700 feet.

When the final glacier melted from the valley about 10,000 years ago, it left behind a lake, dammed by the hill of debris that the ice sheet had pushed ahead of itself as it moved. Fragments of that moraine, as well as others that collected along the edges of the glaciers, still exist in the valley, taking the form of wooded ridges 30-40 feet high. In several places the road into the valley is built on top of these moraines, which may be distinguished by their composition: a mixture of sand, gravel, mud, cobbles and boulders, many of them polished or scarred by the ice.

Debris carried by glaciers and streams had already deposited a thick layer of sediment on the valley floor by the time shallow Lake Yosemite was formed. Over thousands of years the sediment continued to pour in, eventually filling the lake entirely and creating the level valley floor seen today. Seismic surveys conducted by geologists in the 1930s indicate the real floor of the valley, the one scraped into the bedrock by glacial action, lies 2,000 feet below the pleasant meadows of today's Yosemite Valley.

The ice also sculpted the rock walls of the valley, creating sheer faces over which the Merced River's tributary streams—left hanging when the glaciers deepened the valley—now plunged in spectacular falls. Exploiting a pattern of vertical joints in the stone, the glaciers also helped create the sheer face of Half Dome, the best-known example of one of Yosemite's most characteristic geological formations, domes. Although it was never a "whole" dome, Half Dome is believed to have been 20 percent larger before erosion and the plucking of ice weakened the rock on the face above Mirror Lake, causing sheets of stone to drop away.

Half Dome seen from North Dome

Other domes abound in Yosemite, in the vicinity of the valley but also throughout the park, having gained their rounded shape through a process called exfoliation. The domes are slowly expanding, erosion having relieved them of the enormous overlying weight of rock that had pressed down upon them when the granite formed deep beneath the surface. As a dome expands, cracks form within it, creating layers of concentric shells near the surface. Over time those shells, which vary in thickness from less than a foot to as much as 100 feet, break apart and fall off. The process removes projecting corners and angles from the original rock mass, producing a smoothly curving surface.

The geological processes that created the Yosemite landscape are of course still at work. They act slowly, keeping time with the plodding heartbeat of the planet, but not so slowly that their effect cannot be seen within human lifespans. Mirror Lake, for example, a favorite of casual and professional photographers alike earlier in this century, no longer exists. Originally a small pond, it was enlarged by a dam in 1890 to form a lake that cast superb reflections of Half Dome and other nearby cliffs, but had to be dredged frequently to keep it from silting up. That practice was halted in 1971, and today—through the same process that eliminated post-glacial Lake Yosemite—Mirror Lake is mostly meadow.

Ice also continues its work. Water penetrates small cracks in the stone and widens them as it freezes and expands. Repeated cycles of freeze and thaw eventually dislodge fragments from the cliff faces, helping create the huge piles of talus found at the edges of the valley floor. Remnants of glaciers, too, remain high in the rugged Yosemite backcountry, in the shadow of such peaks as Mt. Lyell, Mt. Dana and Mt. Conness. They are frequently the subject of study by scientists who hope to divine in their ebb and flow a hint of the future, an answer to the question of when North America's respite from the ice ages will end.

Human History

Yosemite Valley's first permanent residents were ancestors of the Southern Sierra Miwok, members of the Penutian language group that dominated inland California. They arrived in the area about 3,500 years ago, and by 1200 A.D. had established a culture recognized as the direct predecessor of the one encountered by the first whites to reach the area.

The Miwok occupied Yosemite Valley and the surrounding high country mainly in the summer, when it served as a hunting ground and a means of escaping the heat of the lower elevations. In winter they migrated to the foothills to escape the snow that fell even in the valley and—before the advent of all-weather roads—isolated it from the outside world.

"Miwok" is not the name they gave themselves; in their language the word is merely the term for "people." The Miwok identified themselves by the names of their villages, as did their neighbors. Ahwahne—which means "valley that looks like an open mouth" in the native tongue—was the name of the village occupying the broadest expanse of land in Yosemite Valley, and it came to be used as the name for the entire valley. Those Miwok who lived in the valley were referred to as the Ahwahneeches.

Like many of California's indigenous people, the Southern Sierra Miwok relied on acorns as the staple element in their diet. The nuts, gathered from the black, canyon, live and scrub oaks common in the foothills and the valley, were supplemented by a variety of plants, fish, birds and game.

Dwellings were of two types: conical huts made of slabs of cedar bark lashed to a framework of poles, and partly subterranean lodges featuring domed roofs of thatch and earth erected over pits and supported by upright posts. Clothing, as in many other aboriginal groups in California's mild climate, was scant most of the year, and footgear was worn primarily on long trips or in cold weather. The Miwok were skilled basket makers, and many examples of their work survive in museums.

The Miwok were part of an extensive trade network that sent acorns, baskets and berries over the Sierra in exchange for obsidian, pine nuts and blankets from the Owens Valley Paiutes, and to the coast in exchange for abalone and other shells. Many of the trade routes through the mountains were later followed by white explorers and trappers, and over time the foot trails were transformed into wagon roads and, in some cases, paved highways. Motorists who enter Yosemite National Park from the east on Highway 120, the Tioga Road, follow one such route.

Among those who followed the Indian trade routes was the first white man to see Yosemite Valley. In autumn of 1833 Lt. Joseph Walker of Tennessee led a party of fur trappers from Utah through Nevada and over the Sierra Nevada from east to west—the first such crossing by white men—and camped in deep snow near the edge of Yosemite Valley sometime in November of that year. Although he and his party never entered the valley, his expedition journal's description of the view from the rim leaves no doubt that they were the first whites to see the valley and record their impressions of the vista. Later on that trip Walker and his men became the first whites to encounter the giant sequoias, passing through either the Tuolumne or the Merced Grove northwest of Yosemite Valley.

White men did not return to Yosemite for 16 years, And when they did, it spelled doom for the valley's natives, and the start of a new era in California history.

In 1849 a pair of gold miners following the tracks of a grizzly bear became lost in the mountains along the South Fork Merced River. While searching for a way out, they came across an Indian trail and followed it into the valley. They did not remain long. But they were part of an invading force, a swarm of miners who descended upon the Sierra Nevada following the 1848 discovery of gold at Sutter's Mill on the American River. As the miners scoured the foothills seeking wealth, they displaced—often violently—the natives who called the place home, denying them access to historical hunting and gathering grounds, introducing them to virulent new diseases and shooting them or burning their villages when they refused to get out of the way.

Some Indian groups fought back, and many took to substituting horse flesh for the time-honored food sources the miners were depriving them of. In 1850 a party of Miwok and Yokuts (the dominant tribe of the foothills and Central Valley) raided settlements at Mariposa Creek and on the Fresno River, killing three men. A posse was formed, and an inconclusive battle fought. The disturbance, however, prompted the federal government to intervene, and representatives were sent to contact the Indians of the Yosemite area, persuade them to sign treaties and agree to be resettled—for their own protection—on reservations.

Not surprisingly, many Indians ignored or rejected the offer, preferring to remain in their ancestral homeland. The Ahwahneeches, in particular, refused to even consider leaving their mountain valley. And so in 1851 a detachment of soldiers and volunteers left Mariposa to seek out the "recalcitrant" natives and bring them in—by force, if necessary.

The soldiers and mercenaries succeeded in rounding up hundreds of Miwok, but many of the Ahwahneeches remained out of their grasp for several months, fleeing into the mountains and canyons of the rugged high country. During the search, a detachment of soldiers camped in the valley and gave it its modern name, derived from the Miwok word Yo-ham-i-te, the term for hunters of grizzly bears.

The last of the Ahwahneeches were captured with their chief, Teneiya, on the shore of the lake that now bears his name. The natives had called it Py-we-ack, the Lake of Shining Rocks, in reference to the glacially polished granite surrounding it.

Teneiya and his people were resettled on the Fresno River, and although some of them—including Teneiya—later slipped away and took up residence again in their ancestral homeland, their sojourn was brief. Several were hunted down by whites and executed for killings they may or may not have committed, and the last bands dispersed in 1853, after Teneiya's death. With that event, the Miwok chapter in Yosemite's history ends.

A handful of miners visited the valley during the next two years, and their descriptions of soaring cliffs and plunging waterfalls eventually trickled to the outside world. Among those whose attention they attracted was magazine publisher James Hutchings of San Francisco, who journeyed to the valley in 1855. He brought with him an artist, Thomas Ayres, and the party thoroughly explored Yosemite Valley. Hutchings' written descriptions and Ayres' sketches and drawings were the first widely disseminated depictions of the valley's scenic wonders, and they helped launch the tourist era.

Over the next decade, several trails and wagon roads were extended into the Yosemite Valley region, and the valley acquired its first permanent residents. In 1856 the first hotel was constructed—actually a small cabin. More "improvements" followed, additional hotels, stores and tentlike accommodations being built throughout the valley. Enterprising men felled the valley's pines and cedars for their buildings, constructed wooden causeways over the meadows, and extended staircases alongside the popular waterfalls.

The first halting steps toward preservation came in 1864, when a group of Yosemite enthusiasts persuaded the federal government to deed Yosemite Valley and the Mariposa Grove of sequoias to the state of California for a public park. A commission was formed to administer it, headed by Frederick Law Olmsted, creator of New York's Central Park.

Yosemite's most famous visitor arrived four years later. John Muir stayed only eight days that spring of 1868, but the experience changed the course of his life. He returned the following summer as overseer of a sheep-grazing outfit that sent its flock into the high country, and he used his time to explore and wander. That fall he signed on to work in a sawmill in the valley, and began intensive studies of Yosemite's features and their formation.

Muir would later champion the theory that Yosemite Valley's shape was the result of glacial action, a notion at odds with the opinion of leading geologists of his day, but one that would eventually be substantiated by more sophisticated scientific analysis.

Muir also became a champion of federal preservation of Yosemite and its wonders. Although he initially participated in two of the activities that posed the greatest threat to the area's natural beauty—logging and sheepherding—he could not help but notice the damage being done to the overgrazed meadows and increasingly overdeveloped valley by unregulated human activity. In 1889, urged on by a magazine editor, he began work on a series of articles urging the creation of a Yosemite National Park.

His campaign quickly bore fruit. The articles appeared in *Century* magazine in the summer of 1890, and drew immediate and widespread public support for the park concept. Federal legislation was drafted and quickly passed, and on Oct. 1, 1890 the park was created. It excluded Yosemite Valley and the Mariposa Grove of sequoias, however, which remained under the jurisdiction of the state.

Muir was not content to stop there. In 1895, during a visit to the valley, he became heartsick over the state's lax mismanagement. Dozens of new buildings had sprung up in the six years since his previous visit, and the lush meadows along the Merced River had become little more than trampled, dusty pastures filled with livestock.

Muir enlisted the help of others to found the Sierra Club, created in 1892 with Muir as its first president, and launched a campaign to persuade the federal

The Mariposa Grove Museum near Wawona

government to take control of the valley back from the state. Their battle took a decade, but was successful. In February 1905, California agreed to give up jurisdiction over the valley and the Mariposa Grove of sequoias, which were added the following year to the national park.

The battle to preserve Yosemite didn't end there. In the early 1900s, San Francisco was seeking new sources of water and power, and the eyes of its engineers were drawn eastward, into the Sierra foothills, to the rocky canyon of the Tuolumne River. The city applied to the secretary of the interior for permission to dam the river and create a reservoir in the Hetch Hetchy Valley, despite the fact that it was inside Yosemite National Park.

The infant Sierra Club fought hard, and won temporary victories by persuading the secretary to deny the application. But in 1908 a new interior secretary reconsidered the city's application, and despite arguments that the integrity of a national park should not be defiled for such a dubious purpose—other reservoir sites were available outside the park boundaries—Muir and his supporters nationwide lost the fight in 1913 when Congress passed the Raker Act giving San Francisco the right to inundate the valley.

Muir had described Hetch Hetchy as a second Yosemite, and pictures taken before the dam was built support his description. In many ways it was Yosemite's twin—a broad, flat-bottomed valley with a meandering river flowing across its floor, hemmed in by soaring granite walls down which waterfalls plunged. But the valley now lies beneath a lake formed by O'Shaughnessy Dam, which began sending water and power to the city by the bay in 1934. Muir died in 1914, the year after he lost the battle to keep Hetch Hetchy unspoiled.

The fight, however, had transformed the Sierra Club into a more vocal, powerful lobbying voice for wilderness preservation. In 1916, at the urging of the club and its growing corps of supporters, Congress established the National Park Service, and gave it control over Yosemite and the handful of other parks and monuments under federal control..

The following decades would see changes in the facilities and services offered in the valley, and enormous growth in the number of visitors. Nearly 3.5 million people travel into the valley each year now, a far cry from the 48 sightseers who made their way by horseback into the valley in 1855. Instead of Miwok trails or rough wagon roads, today's visitors follow year-round highways, and when they arrive they find pizza parlors, video rental shops, swimming pools, a jail, a courthouse—in all, 1,300 buildings, as well as 30 miles of paved roads, eight miles of paved bike paths and 17 acres of parking lots. On peak midsummer days, the valley is host to 20,000 people.

But despite the traffic, the occasional smog, the noise and the crowding, Yosemite still possesses the scenic majesty that drew Muir and those first hardy sightseers, the same powerful pull on the senses that led Teneiya and his Ahwahneeches to risk death rather than leave. The valley's first inhabitants would not recognize their old hunting and camping grounds, but casting their gaze upward, they would still recognize the gleaming granite walls, which change only with the passage of centuries, and the plunging waterfalls that dance on the wind as long as the rain and the snow continue to fall.

Plants and Animals

Elevations within Yosemite National Park range from around 2,000 feet at its western boundary to more than 13,000 feet along its eastern edge, where the crest of the Sierra Nevada soars jaggedly above the Mono Basin. With such a wide range of altitudes, the park encompasses an equally broad variety of plant and animal communities. More than 230 species of birds, 80 species of mammals and 1,400 species of shrubs, trees and flowers have been recorded in the park.

At the lowest elevation, along the park boundary at El Portal, at Hetch Hetchy and along parts of the Wawona and Big Oak Flat roads, lies the foothill woodland community, the realm of oaks and digger pines. California buckeye, which in springtime sends forth long, showy clusters of white flowers, manzanita and other hardy shrubs such as toyon and redbud, also may be found there.

With its abundant food sources, primarily acorns, berries and the seeds of grasses, the foothill woodland supports a large and varied population of wildlife. Resident species include the gray and California ground squirrels, Merriam's chipmunk, raccoon, striped and spotted skunks, coyote, gray fox, bobcat and ringtail. Mule deer are common only in winter and spring, when they are forced down from their high-elevation haunts by heavy snow. They are the chief prey of mountain lions, who follow them into the foothills but are seldom seen. Dozens of species of birds also call the foothill woodland home, including the screech, long-eared and great horned owls, red-tailed and Cooper's hawks, California quail, and acorn, downy and Nuttall's woodpeckers.

Starting at about 3000 feet on the western slope, the foothill woodland gives way to the mixed coniferous forest. This is divided into several zones, each dominated by a characteristic community of plants.

At the lowest zone lies the ponderosa-pine forest, dominated by its namesake, and including black oak, incense-cedar, white fir and sugar pine. Along streams, trees include cottonwood, dogwood, alder and maple. Throughout, the understory includes manzanita, buckbrush and deer brush. The floor of Yosemite Valley offers a good example of this type of plant community, which flourishes during the long, warm summer and relatively mild winter typical of elevations between 3,000 and 4,000 feet. Skunks, raccoons, coyotes, several varieties of squirrels, and black bears—the bane of many campgrounds in the park—reside here, as do dozens of species of birds. Perhaps the most familiar of these is the raucous Steller's jay, recognizable by its vivid blue plumage and the black crest on its head, a bird so bold it will grab food right off a camper's plate if given the chance.

At about 4,000 feet the average year-round temperature is significantly cooler, precipitation is greater and winter snows linger longer. Ponderosa pine gives way to its close cousin, Jeffrey pine, and the white-fir forest takes over. Extending up to about 7,000 feet on the west slope, the white-fir forest includes the sugar pines and incense-cedars of the ponderosa forest, but also Douglas-fir and the most famous of the Sierra's plants, the giant sequoia.

Yosemite National Park contains three of the 75 remaining sequoia groves: The Mariposa Grove, 35 miles south of the valley, near the park entrance at Wawona, the largest of the three, contains about 500 mature trees scattered over 250 acres. The smaller Tuolumne and Merced groves are near Crane Flat, northwest of Yosemite Valley near the Big Oak Flat Road.

Sequoias flourish only on moist, unglaciated slopes between 4,500 and 8,000 feet, and are the most massive living things on the planet. They require under-

National Park Service

Lodgepole pines

brush-clearing fires to germinate, and are themselves all but impervious to flame when mature. They also resist decay, because of the natural concentration of tannin in their bark and wood, and the fallen giants may remain intact on the forest floor for over a century.

At its upper end the white fir forest blends into the red fir forest, often imperceptibly. At this elevation, about 7,000-8,000 feet, the Sierra receives its heaviest snowfall, averaging 400-500 inches a year. Red firs require deep, well-drained soil, and large stands may be found in Yosemite for miles along the Tioga Road. Red firs form dense stands that generally crowd out other plants, although isolated groves of lodgepole pine may also be found among them.

Lodgepoles are the dominant plant at this elevation in areas of thinner soil and harsher exposure than the red fir can tolerate, such as the glaciated ridges, valleys and lake basins of the Yosemite high country. Lodgepoles cluster thickly along the edges of Tuolumne Meadows in Yosemite, the largest subalpine meadow in the Sierra, and elsewhere form thick stands that prevent undergrowth by blocking the sunlight.

Above the red fir-lodgepole zone is the subalpine forest, extending from 8,000 feet to treeline, which is at about 12,000 feet in the southern Sierra, 10,000 feet in the north. Lodgepole persists here, and is joined by whitebark pine, mountain hemlock and foxtail pine. There are few deciduous trees in this cold region, where the growing season may be no more than a couple of months long and where snow may fall at almost any time of year. Quaking aspen is the notable exception, found as high as 10,000 feet in sheltered sites with ample water. Low-lying shrubs such as sagebrush and currant form thick mats in open areas, hugging the ground to escape the wind and conserve warmth.

Above this lies the alpine zone, a barren, rocky world where only dwarf herbs, grasses and shrubs survive. It is the environment of the rocky mountaintops of Yosemite, especially along the east boundary, which follows the Sierra crest. A surprising number of wildflowers may be found here, including sky pilot, columbine, and several varieties of penstemon, especially in boulder fields where crannies in the rocks provide shelter and reflect the sunlight. Animals, including humans, are only temporary visitors here.

Facilities

The first structure of any permanence built by whites in Yosemite was a crude hotel; in many ways this emphasis on accommodating visitors has never waned. Although most of the park is open only to travelers on foot or horseback, amenities for less adventurous visitors abound, ranging from walk-in campgrounds to luxurious hotels, from photo shops and pizza parlors to grocery stores, souvenir shops and gas stations.

Roads

Access to Yosemite National Park is primarily from three directions: From the south, on Highway 41 from Fresno; from the west, on Highway 140 from Merced or Highway 120 from Manteca; and from the east, on Highway 120 from Lee Vining, a small town at the junction of 120 and U.S. 395.

Highway 120, also known as the Tioga Road, crosses the park from east to west, and includes the highest paved highway crossing of the Sierra crest, at 9,945-foot Tioga Pass at the eastern park boundary. Highways 41 and 140 are open year-round, but the Tioga Road is closed at Crane Flat in winter, generally from November to May. The closing and opening dates vary from year to year, depending on snowfall, and it is best to call the park's recorded road and weather information line before making plans to drive over Tioga Pass.

Other park highways include the Glacier Point Road, which leads from Highway 41 at Chinquapin to a magnificent viewpoint overlooking Yosemite Valley, the Hetch Hetchy road, which splits from Highway 120 just outside the park near the Big Oak Flat entrance and leads to Hetch Hetchy Reservoir, and the Old Big Oak Flat road, which leads through the Tuolumne Grove of giant sequoias northwest of Yosemite Valley.

Visitor Centers

Maps, books, postcards, prints, wilderness permits and general park information are available at four visitor centers in the park. The main visitor center is in Yosemite Valley, and is open daily year-round. A second center is in Tuolumne Meadows, and is open from late spring until late September. A smaller information center is located at Wawona, near the park's south entrance, off the Chilnualna Falls Road. The Wawona station is open year-round; the Tuolumne Meadows station is closed in winter.

A $5 entrance fee is collected at all park entrances and is good for seven days. Free Golden Age passes to the national parks are available for those 62 and older who are U.S. citizens or permanent residents. Annual passes to the park are $15, and a Golden Eagle Passport, good for unlimited entry to all elements of the national park system during a calendar year, is $25.

Campgrounds

There are 17 campgrounds in Yosemite National Park, containing more than 1,900 sites. Some are open year-round, and most of those in the valley are available only by reservation. An alphabetical listing follows.

Backpackers Walk-in: In Yosemite Valley. Elevation 4000 feet. 25 sites. Flush toilets, tap water. Closed in winter. Open only to visitors without vehicles. First come, first served; two-night maximum. Fee is $2 per night per person.

Bridalveil Creek: 25 miles from Yosemite Valley on the Glacier Point Road. Elevation 7200 feet. 110 sites. Flush toilets, tap water. Closed in winter. First come, first served. Fee is $7 per night.

Crane Flat: 17 miles from Yosemite Valley on Highway 120, near the Tioga Road turnoff. Elevation 6191 feet. 166 sites. Flush toilets, tap water. Closed in winter. Reservations required. $10 per night.

Hetch Hetchy backpackers: At Hetch Hetchy reservoir, 38 miles from Yosemite Valley at end of Hetch Hetchy Road. Elevation 3800 feet. 25 sites. Flush toilets, tap water. Open year-round. Walk-in only; wilderness permits required. First come, first served. $2 per person per night.

Hodgdon Meadow: On Highway 120 near Big Oak Flat, 25 miles from Yosemite Valley. Elevation 4875 feet. 105 sites. Flush toilets, tap water. Open year-round; reservations required in summer. $10 per night in summer; $7 in winter.

Lower Pines: In Yosemite Valley. Elevation 4000 feet. 172 sites. Flush toilets, tap water. Open year-round. Reservations required. $12 per night.

Lower River: In Yosemite Valley. Elevation 4000 feet. 138 sites. Flush toilets, tap water. Closed in winter. Reservations required. $12 per night.

North Pines: In Yosemite Valley. Elevation 4000 feet. 85 sites. Flush toilets, tap water. Closed in winter. Reservations required. $12 per night.

Porcupine Flat: On Tioga Road, 38 miles from Yosemite Valley. Elevation 8100 feet. 52 sites. Pit toilets, stream water (must be boiled or treated). Closed in winter. First come, first served. Recreational-vehicle access limited to front section. $4 per night.

Sunnyside Walk-in: In Yosemite Valley. Elevation 4000 feet. 35 sites. Flush toilets, tap water. Closed in winter. First come, first served. Vehicles not allowed in campsites. $2 per person per night.

Tamarack Flat: Off Tioga Road east of junction with Big Oak Flat Road, 23 miles from Yosemite Valley. Elevation 6315 feet. 52 sites. Pit toilets, stream water (boil or treat). Closed in winter. Three-mile access road not suitable for RV's or trailers. $4 per night.

Tuolumne Meadows: On Tioga Road, 55 miles from Yosemite Valley. Elevation 8600 feet. 314 sites. Flush toilets, tap water. Closed in winter. Half the sites by reservation only; half available same day. $10 per night. 25 walk-in sites reserved for backpackers and other visitors without vehicles; fee $2 per person per night.

Upper Pines: In Yosemite Valley. Elevation 4000 feet. 238 sites. Flush toilets, tap water. Closed in winter. Reservations required. $12 per night.

Upper River: In Yosemite Valley. Elevation 4000 feet. 124 sites. Flush toilets, tap water. Closed in winter. Reservations required. $12 per night.

Wawona: On Highway 41 in Wawona, 27 miles from Yosemite Valley at the south entrance to the park. Elevation 4000 feet. 100 sites. Flush toilets, tap water. Open year-round. First come, first served. $7 per night.

White Wolf: Off Tioga Road, 31 miles from Yosemite Valley. 87 sites. Flush toilets, tap water. Closed in winter. First come, first served. $7 per night.

Yosemite Creek: Off Tioga Road, 35 miles from Yosemite Valley. 75 sites. Pit toilets, stream water. Closed in winter. Five-mile access road unsuitable for RV's and trailers. First come, first served. $4 per night.

Park campgrounds fill on most summer weekends and on all holidays. Chances of finding a site are better mid-week and during the off season. The park is also surrounded by the Sierra, Inyo, Toiyabe and Stanislaus national forests, each of which has campgrounds near enough to serve as backup destinations should Yosemite's accommodations be full. In addition, the Forest Service generally permits camping anywhere in undeveloped areas of the forest, although campfires are generally prohibited outside developed sites during the summer wildfire season and require special permits the rest of the year.

The nearest developed national forest campgrounds are at Saddlebag Lake, Ellery Lake, Tioga Lake and Lee Vining Creek off Highway 120 east of Tioga Pass; Summerdale, on Highway 41 just outside the park's south entrance; and Indian Flat, on Highway 120 west of El Portal on the park's west side. Contact the appropriate Forest Service district office for maps and camping information.

Food, Gas and Lodging

Gas stations and markets are located in Yosemite Valley, Crane Flat, Tuolumne Meadows, Wawona and El Portal. Several restaurants and snack bars are located throughout the valley, as well as at Tuolumne Meadows, White Wolf, Glacier Point, and Wawona. Lodging in the park is available year-round at the Ahwahnee Hotel and Yosemite Lodge in the valley, and the Wawona Hotel at Wawona; summertime accommodations are also available at Tuolumne Lodge in Tuolumne Meadows. Tent cabins are also available only in summer at Curry Village.

Other Attractions

Yosemite National Park offers one of the most extensive interpretive programs of any national park, with dozens of ranger-led walks, campfire programs, talks and other activities scheduled each week during the summer months. Consult the park visitor guide for a current schedule.

The park also offers a wide variety of activities besides hiking and driving, including horseback riding, rock-climbing classes, cross-country and downhill skiing, snowshoeing, open-air tram tours and bicycling. Bicycles may be rented at Curry Village (summer only) and Yosemite Lodge (year-round), and stables are located in the valley and at Wawona, White Wolf and Tuolumne Meadows. The latter two are closed in winter.

For a complete list of activities consult the park visitor guide.

Phone Numbers and Addresses

To make campsite reservations (see the preceding chapter for a list of campgrounds where reservations are required), call DESTINET at (800) 436-7275. Reservations may be made up to eight weeks in advance, and you will need to know your credit-card number and expiration date, the number of people in your group, your first, second and third choices of arrival date and number of nights, and the type of camping equipment you will be using.

Campground reservations may also be made by mail at the following address:

DESTINET
P.O. Box 85705
San Diego, CA 92138-5705

Recorded weather, road and general park information is available 24 hours a day at (209) 372-0200. The recording is updated each morning.

To make reservations at any of the lodges or hotels in the park, call (209) 252-4848.

For information about camping in the surrounding national forests, contact the following U.S. Forest Service district offices:

Inyo National Forest
Mono Lake Ranger District: (619) 647-6525

Sierra National Forest
Bass Lake Ranger District: (209) 683-4665
Mariposa Ranger District: (209) 966-3638

Stanislaus National Forest
Groveland Ranger District: (209) 962-7825   ■

*When I first enjoyed
this superb view, one glowing
April day, from the summit of the
Pacheco Pass, the Central Valley, but little
trampled or plowed as yet, was one furred,
rich sheet of golden compositæ, and the
luminous wall of the mountains shone in all its glory.
Then it seemed to me the Sierra should be called not the
Nevada, or Snowy Range, but the Range of Light. And
after ten years spent in the heart of it, rejoicing and
wondering, bathing in its glorious floods of light, seeing
the sunbursts of morning among the icy peaks,
the noonday radiance on the trees and rocks and snow,
the flush of the alpenglow, and a thousand dashing
waterfalls with their marvelous abundance of irised
spray, it still seems to me above all others
the Range of Light,
the most divinely beautiful of all
the mountain-chains I have ever seen.
—John Muir*
The Mountains of California

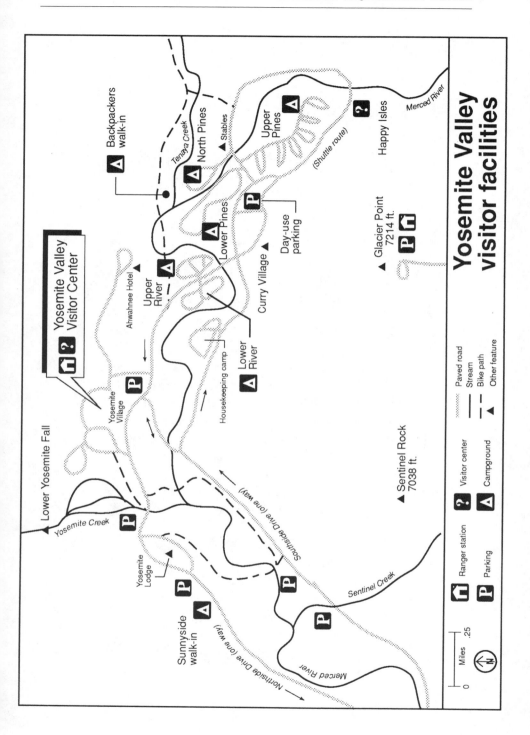

Yosemite Valley
visitor facilities

Day Hikes in Yosemite National Park

Trails of Yosemite Valley

Yosemite National Park draws about 3.5 million visitors each year, and in the summer it sometimes seems as though all of them were in the valley at one time. As the scenic heart of the park—as well as the entire Sierra Nevada—Yosemite Valley suffers under incredible pressure from visitors, who crowd its roads, trails, parking lots, campgrounds and hotels to catch a glimpse of its astonishing features.

As a result, the valley takes on many of the aspects of an urban environment, especially on holiday weekends. Traffic jams develop, smog levels rise, crime soars, and the overall experience is about as peaceful as standing on a Los Angeles street corner at rush hour. Even the trails can be crowded, especially the short ones leading to the best-known views of Yosemite's familiar features.

Still, the valley's trails offer the best chance to get close to and truly appreciate the heart-stopping grandeur of Yosemite's towering granite monoliths, its leaping waterfalls, its meadows and streams. Because of its low elevation—around 4000 feet—the valley is open year-round, and many of its trails are snowless most of the winter. March and April are good times to visit, because the waterfalls will be near full strength—many all but dry up in summer—the crowds have not yet arrived, and the days are cool enough for pleasant hiking.

The following trails vary from easy and level to arduous and steep. If you hike all of them, you will get close-up views of all the valley's most magnificent features, and you'll be able to enjoy their charms at your leisure. As you'll quickly discover, it beats the heck out of driving around the valley slowing only to take quick snapshots out the car window as views of Half Dome and Yosemite Falls slip past. ■

Hike #26: Lodge Loop

Distance	5.5 miles
Level of difficulty	Easy
Child rating	10 and up
Starting elevation	3990 feet
Highest point on trail	4000 feet
Topographic maps	El Capitan, Half Dome 7.5';
	Yosemite 15'
Guidebook map	16

Most of Yosemite's visitors tour the valley by auto, catching hurried glimpses of its great geological landmarks while dodging motorized traffic or jostling for space in crowded turnouts. This hike, especially if paired with the West Loop, described as Hike #29, offers a close-up view of many valley features in a far less crowded setting and at a leisurely pace.

The hike begins at the parking lot for Sunnyside walk-in campground, situated on Northside Drive almost across the road from Yosemite Lodge. Day-use parking is not allowed in the campground lot, but is available at the lodge. Walk north through the campground parking area and turn left when you meet the trail, about 50 few yards uphill past the pavement's end.

The path leads southwest, through the typical valley plant community of oak trees and incense-cedars. The trail crosses the road at 0.3 mile and skirts the edge of Leidig Meadow before reaching the banks of the Merced River, which it then parallels. The cottonwoods and willows beside the water frame lovely views of Half Dome to the east.

The trail reaches the Sentinel Beach picnic area at 0.7 mile, and the Yellow Pine picnic area at 0.8 mile, the latter named for the trees that predominate in the vicinity. Meandering between river's edge and ponderosa-pine forest, the trail takes a more westerly course at 1.3 miles and offers the first of several increasingly awe-inspiring views of El Capitan.

The trail next skirts the edge of a dump site, used between the 1880s and the 1920s, and then buried and forgotten. In 1964, however, the flooding Merced altered its course and cut through the old dump, exposing and carrying the old trash downstream. In 1991 the Park Service began digging up the old dump, sifting through the trash for items of historical interest and removing the remainder for reburial outside the valley. The streamside part of the dump was refilled, and the bank replanted with willows and cottonwoods to stem erosion.

At 1.8 miles the trail passes the El Capitan Picnic Area, and at 2.3 miles reaches Devil's Elbow, a sharp curve in the river's course where another picnic spot is located. This is a good place to pause and take in the spectacle of El Capitan, looming overhead. The gleaming stone rises 3000 feet from the valley floor, and is among the largest exposed granite monoliths in the world. Its size overwhelms the senses, making it difficult to truly appreciate the scale. A favorite with climbers, the cliff is also home to one of Yosemite Valley's two nesting pairs of peregrine falcons, an endangered species making a slow comeback after being driven nearly to extinction by the use of pesticides such as DDT.

Past the picnic area, leave the trail and follow the road east across the bridge over the Merced, and pick up the trail again at the river's edge. Follow it half a mile to the Cathedral Beach Picnic Area. Cross the road here and follow the trail a short distance southeast, turning left when you reach the junction at 3 miles.

From here the trail leads for 2 miles along the foot of the soaring cliffs that form the south wall of the valley, passing among boulders fallen from the heights. Views north include Upper and Lower Yosemite Falls and the Three Brothers, a striking set of parallel peaks formed by giant, parallel joints in the stone. The feature is named for the three sons of Chief Teneiya, last leader of the Ahwahneeches, who were captured nearby in 1851 by soldiers sent to relocate the valley's native inhabitants.

At 4.5 miles, the trail crosses icy Sentinel Creek, dry in summer, which feeds Sentinel Fall high above. A quarter mile farther the trail reaches a junction with the Four Mile Trail, a strenuous but highly scenic path leading from the valley floor to Glacier Point 3,200 feet above.

At 5 miles the trail leads near the edge of the road and reaches a junction across from the Swinging Bridge Picnic Area. Turn left, cross the road and walk through the large, shaded picnic grounds. Take the bridge cross the Merced River to Leidig Meadow, which provides one of the best viewpoints on the valley floor. Face west and the panorama includes the Three Brothers and Cathedral Rocks; turn around and the view encompasses North Dome, Royal Arches, Washington Column, Clouds Rest and Half Dome. The meadow was named after George and Isabella Leidig, who operated a hotel below Sentinel Rock, facing Yosemite Falls. Built in 1869, the hotel was torn down in 1888. The Leidigs' son, Charles, born the year the hotel was built, was the first white child born in the valley.

The trail follows the paved bike path along the meadow's edge to Yosemite Lodge. Follow the lodge driveway back to Northside Drive, and cross it to the Sunnyside Campground parking area at 5.5 miles. ■

Hike #27: Nevada Fall

Distance	8.5 miles
Level of difficulty	Strenuous
Child rating	10 and up
Starting elevation	3980 feet
Highest point on trail	5880 feet
Topographic maps	Half Dome 7.5'; Yosemite Valley 15'
Guidebook map	17

Yosemite's waterfalls are its glory, decorating the massive granite cliff faces with rainbows and breeze-blown pennants of mist. Formed with the help of glaciers, which carved the main valley deeper than the side canyons and left the Merced River's tributary streams hanging thousands of feet above it, they are at their most spectacular early in the season when runoff from melting snow is high.

This hike leads up the popular Mist Trail past Vernal Fall to the top of Nevada Fall and loops back along the John Muir Trail. In winter or early spring parts of both trails may be closed by ice or snow, so check with park rangers before setting out. The hike involves a steep ascent along sheer cliffs, and is not advised for hikers with small children or people afraid of heights.

One more word of caution: The river is swift, strong and icy, and under no circumstances should hikers go wading above the falls. The danger is simple and unarguable: If you slip and fall, you will die.

The trail begins at Happy Isles, at the southeast end of Yosemite Valley. Park in the day-use parking lot at Curry Village and follow the paved shuttle-bus route, closed to private vehicles, 1 mile to Happy Isles. In spring and summer, you can ride the free shuttle to stop #16. The mileages in this description are calculated from the day-use parking lot.

The trail leads to the right from the shuttle route as it nears the Merced River, passing the Happy Isles Nature Center (closed in winter) before crossing the river on a broad wooden bridge. Then the trail leads south, passing a spring-filled cistern, and climbs steeply through a mixed forest of oak and California laurel into the glacier-widened Merced River canyon. At 1.2 miles the trail offers a view back across the valley to Yosemite Falls.

The trail is paved in many places, testimony to its popularity, and even in the off-season you will find yourself sharing it with many other hikers of widely varying levels of experience and stamina. This is a good place to remember proper trail etiquette: If you're moving slowly, step aside periodically to let faster parties pass; if you're powering up the hill, show a little patience with those in the slow lane.

At 1.4 miles you catch glimpses of wispy Illilouette Fall, up-canyon to your right. Now the trail rounds Sierra Point and leads almost due east into the Merced

River canyon, continuing its ascent. At 2 miles it reaches a bridge, which offers a view of Vernal Fall, and crosses the Merced, climbing now above its south bank. Immediately after crossing the bridge, the trail reaches a junction. The John Muir Trail leads to the right; you proceed to the left, on the Mist Trail.

As you approach the base of Vernal Fall, the trail grows slippery with mist. It also steepens, climbing a series of rock stair-steps that ascend to the lip of the fall at 2.3 miles. Here the trail leads onto a broad, sunny expanse of rock, encircled by railings, which offers a view into the gorge. Vernal Fall plummets 317 feet into this gorge.

The trail continues along the south bank of the river, passing again through oak and incense-cedar woodland dotted with boulders. Just upstream from the fall it passes the Silver Apron, a broad, slick rock chute over which the Merced spreads in a glittering fan. Steepening, the path resumes its ascent, reaching a junction at 2.5 miles. The right branch leads to the Muir Trail; steer to the left and cross the Merced on a small footbridge.

Ahead you can see a pair of soaring granite monoliths: Mt. Broderick on the left, Liberty Cap on the right. The trail levels out for a short distance, and then begins yet another steep climb at 2.7 miles. At 3 miles it reaches the base of Nevada Fall, which fills the air with mist and thunder.

The last, grueling section starts at 3.1 miles, with a resumption of the granite stairway, which leads up the flank of Liberty Cap and reaches a trail junction at 3.5 miles. To the left, the trail leads to Half Dome. Bear right, leveling out and turning southwest to follow the river bank to the lip of 594-foot-high Nevada Fall at 3.7 miles. The area around the fall is level and pleasantly forested, and makes a good picnic spot. Remember to stay out of the river.

The trail continues southwest across a bridge that spans the river at the lip of the fall, and at 4 miles reaches a junction with the Panorama Trail. Bear right, following the Muir Trail past a gate that may bar it early in the season. Just past the gate the trail clings to the side of a steep rock face, which may be drenched by meltwater falling from the heights above. Across the valley to the northwest you can see Yosemite Falls.

At 5.1 miles the trail reaches Clark Point and a junction with a trail leading back down to the Mist Trail. To the east is a magnificent view of Nevada Fall.

Bear left at the junction, continuing the often steep descent into the Merced canyon. At 6.4 miles the trail forks again, with a horse path leading to the left and back toward Curry Village. Turn right and continue downhill to your junction with the Mist Trail, at 6.5 miles. Bear left and retrace your steps to Happy Isles at 7.5 miles. From here it is a mile back to your car at Curry Village. ■

Hike #28: Tenaya Canyon Loop

Distance	4.8 miles
Level of difficulty	Easy
Child rating	5 and up
Starting elevation	3980 feet
Highest point on trail	4160 feet
Topographic maps	Half Dome, Yosemite Falls 7.5', Yosemite Valley, Hetch Hetchy 15'
Guidebook map	17

This gentle hike leads past the former site of Mirror Lake, still labeled as such on maps even though the lake ceased to exist in the late 1980s, and then passes the foot of Half Dome before looping back across Tenaya Creek.

The trail begins at Tenaya Bridge, where the bike path and shuttle-bus routes cross Tenaya Creek at the east end of Yosemite Valley. If you are staying in Upper, Lower or North Pines campground, you can walk from your campsite. Alternatives are to leave your car in the day-use parking area next to Curry Village, or to ride the free shuttle bus to stop #17 in summer or #19 in winter. If you park at Curry Village or walk from the campgrounds, add 1 mile to the round trip.

Follow the paved road from Curry Village or the campgrounds, across the Merced River to the stables, where the road is closed to private motor vehicles. Bear left at the fork in the road, and pick up the trail on the right immediately before you cross Tenaya Bridge. The trail forks almost immediately; take the left branch along the south bank of Tenaya Creek.

The trail passes between mossy boulders in the dense shade of oaks and incense-cedars. To your left, across glacier-widened Tenaya Canyon, Washington Column and North Dome are visible. At 0.8 mile, the trail reaches the edge of a marshy area that was once Mirror Lake.

The shallow lake was created by a rockfall that dammed Tenaya Creek near this spot. The dam was enlarged by human hands in the late 1800s, creating a fine reflective pool that captured images of Mt. Watkins and Half Dome. The lake quickly became clogged with sediment, however, and only annual dredging kept it from turning into a meadow. Dredging was halted in the 1970s, however, and the creek now meanders past wide sandbars through a soggy meadow.

The trail leads along the east edge of the former lake, and returns to thick forest at 1.4 miles. Ahead and to the left, rising above the northwest rim of Tenaya Canyon, towers distinctively rounded Basket Dome. Continuing on a mostly level path, we reach a bridge crossing Tenaya Creek at 2.1 miles. From the middle of the span, there are views upstream to Quarter Domes, which lie northeast of Half Dome.

Beyond the stream, the trail leads slightly downhill, leveling out at 2.5 miles as it reaches a junction with the Snow Creek Trail to the right. Continue straight ahead, returning to the Mirror Lake meadow at 3.1 miles. On this side of the meadow is the spot that formerly provided the famous view of Mt. Watkins reflected in the still waters of the former lake. Hikers can still find their way to the viewpoint and gaze northeast at the 8,500-foot bulk of the mountain, but they will have to be satisfied with the limpid stream and its paddling ducks in the foreground.

A few yards past the meadow the trail forks. Bear right and follow the trail across the paved bike path, paralleling it as you continue gently downhill to another fork at 4.2 miles. Take the left branch and follow it back to the Tenaya Bridge and thence to your starting point.   ■

Clouds Rest towers above Tenaya Canyon

Hike #29: West Valley Loop

Distance	4 miles
Level of difficulty	Easy
Child rating	5 and up
Starting elevation	3960 feet
Highest point on trail	4120 feet
Topographic maps	El Capitan 7.5'; Yosemite 15'
Guidebook map	18

Close-up views of awe-inspiring El Capitan, Bridalveil Fall and Cathedral Rocks await hikers on this mostly level circuit of the west end of Yosemite Valley.

The hike begins at the Devil's Elbow Picnic Area, on Northside Drive about 2 miles west of Yosemite Lodge. The trail leaves the north side of the road a few yards west of the picnic area, and passes the foot of El Capitan. At 0.4 mile it crosses a dry creekbed and reaches a junction with a faint spur trail leading downhill to the road. Continue straight, and cross tiny Ribbon Creek at 0.6 mile. A few yards beyond, the trail reaches an abandoned road now used as a trail. Uphill, this path leaves the valley and leads eventually to Tamarack Flat. We follow it downhill to where it connects with a trail about 10 yards from Northside Drive.

Take this trail, which leads to the right. For the next 1.5 miles, the trail leads through oak and ponderosa pine as it parallels the road, offering occasional views across the valley to the craggy spires of Cathedral Rocks, Leaning Tower, Bridalveil Fall, and the broad-browed cliff punctuated by Dewey, Crocker, Stanford and Old Inspiration points.

At 2 miles the trail descends slightly to the road and then follows it across the Merced River on Pohono Bridge. "Pohono"—which means "puffing wind"—is the name the Ahwahneeches gave to Bridalveil Fall, which sways and twists in the breeze.

The trail resumes to your left just across the bridge, and parallels the road to the edge of Bridalveil Meadow. The trail formerly crossed the meadow, but the route has been blocked by the Park Service in an effort to prevent damage to the fragile meadow plant life by the impact of thousands of booted feet. As you reach the meadow, move to the road's shoulder and follow it ¼ mile until you reach the parking area for the short trail to the base of Bridalveil Fall, near the intersection of Southside Drive and Wawona Road. Cross to the south side of Wawona Road here—the trek to the fall is a worthwhile ½-mile round trip if you have the time—and pick up the trail again as it heads east from the end of the parking area toward Curry Village.

The trail climbs moderately here, ascending the slope at the base of Cathedral Rocks before heading back downhill toward the road. At 3 miles the trail levels out and parallels the road, offering fine views across the valley toward El Capitan and the Three Brothers. At 3.5 miles, turn left at a junction and follow the spur to the park road at the Cathedral Beach Picnic Area. Cross the road, walk through the picnic area, and pick up the trail again at the bank of the river. Follow it ½ mile back to the bridge over the river. Cross the bridge and follow the edge of the road back to your starting point at the Devil's Elbow Picnic Area.   ■

El Capitan dominates the west Valley

Hike #30: Yosemite Falls

Distance	7 miles
Level of difficulty	Strenuous
Child rating	10 and up
Starting elevation	3990 feet
Highest point on trail	6600 feet
Topographic maps	Yosemite Falls 7.5';
	Yosemite, Hetch Hetchy Reservoir 15'
Guidebook map	16

The route to the top of North America's tallest waterfall is not an easy one, but it offers unmatched views and a chance to walk in the spray of the plummeting stream. Despite its steepness and elevation gain, the trail is heavily used, so prepare for congestion and be patient with your fellow hikers.

In late summer the falls are reduced to a trickle, so the best time to hike this trail is in springtime, when snowmelt pushes the falls to their most extravagant. Because it climbs a south-facing cliff, the trail is likely to be clear of snow earlier than other valley footpaths.

The trailhead is at Sunnyside walk-in campground. Park across the road at Yosemite Lodge and walk north through the Sunnyside campground parking area. When you reach a trail, turn left and walk a few yards to the signed junction with the Yosemite Falls trail.

The trail begins climbing immediately, switchbacking steeply up the talus slope through big oaks. It's a dusty climb, and a hot one on a sunny afternoon. The ascent grows more moderate after 0.75 mile, and at 1 mile the trail reaches Columbia Rock, an open viewpoint that provides exciting vistas of the valley floor 1000 feet below, as well as a clear view of Half Dome and Quarter Domes to the east.

At 1.4 miles the trail approaches Lower Yosemite Fall, and the air is filled with mist and spray. If the light is right, vivid rainbows dance above the rocks at the base of the fall, and the flying spray turns the stones slick and treacherous underfoot. Lower Yosemite Fall drops 320 feet, and combines with the middle cascades (675 feet) and Upper Yosemite Fall (1,430 feet) to produce a total height of 2,425 feet.

The steep switchbacks resume as the trail begins to lead up a cleft in the cliffs toward the rim of the valley. Soon trees are left behind, and the trail crosses stony slopes that are periodically bombarded by rockfalls. It is not a place to tarry, although the view is increasingly spectacular.

The trail tops out at 3 miles and bends east, reaching a junction with the Eagle Peak trail. Bear right, following the trail downhill to the bank of Yosemite Creek.

It is possible, though extremely dangerous, to work your way to the edge of the cliff above the lip of the fall, but there's no good spot to see the creek actually tumble over the cliff's edge. Remember to stay well back from the creek itself, as the water is swift and icy, and the boulders worn and slick. A misstep would send you plunging over the edge.

The trail continues across the creek on a bridge and climbs 0.75 mile to Yosemite Point, another scenic viewpoint. The view from the banks of Yosemite Creek is quite spectacular, however, reaching above the valley rim to the serrated, ice-cloaked peaks of the Clark Range away to the southeast. The level, lightly forested area surrounding the creek makes a pleasant spot to picnic and rest up before tackling the bone-jarring descent back to the trailhead. ∎

Yosemite Falls

The Cathedral Range above the Tuolumne River

Trails of the Tioga Road Area

Winding 46 miles through the heart of Yosemite National Park and thence to Lee Vining, the Tioga Road offers one of the great scenic drives in the Sierra Nevada. From its western junction with the Big Oak Flat Road at Crane Flat, it rises through forests of lodgepole pine and red fir, traverses the spectacular glaciated granite above Tenaya Canyon, and winds along the stony shore of Tenaya Lake before reaching Tuolumne Meadows, the largest subalpine meadow in the Sierra. Past the meadow it climbs again, topping out at 9,945-foot Tioga Pass, the highest automobile crossing of the Sierra Nevada. East of the pass the road drops steeply to meet Highway 395 at Lee Vining.

For much of its length, the road follows an old Indian trading route known as the Mono Trail. Archaeological evidence indicates that about 4,000 years ago the Miwoks of the western slope used this route to exchange acorns, berries, beads, arrows and baskets for pine nuts, moth larvae, fly pupae, salt, obsidian, rabbit and buffalo skins, and baskets provided by the Mono Indians of the east.

The trail was later followed by white men, including the exploring party of Joseph Reddeford Walker, who in 1833 became the first whites to glimpse Yosemite Valley. In 1852 a group of soldiers pursuing Indians sought for the murder of a pair of prospectors followed the trail past Tenaya Lake and into Bloody Canyon on the east slope. Along the way the group's leader, Lt. Tredwell Moore, spotted some mineral outcroppings and brought samples of gold ore back with him to Mariposa.

His discovery brought more prospectors, although no commercially viable concentrations of ore would be found until 1877. In 1878, claims were established on Tioga Hill, a mining district was formed, and in 1882 work began on the Great Sierra Mine, located north of Tioga Pass. The town of Bennettville sprang up nearby, serving as the company's headquarters. Teams hauled thousand of pounds of mining equipment over the mountains, through deep snow, persuading the mining company's directors that a wagon road across the mountains was needed.

The Great Sierra Consolidated Silver Company approved construction of the road in 1882. Engineers surveyed a route from Crocker's Station (a little over a mile north of the Big Oak Flat park entrance) through Aspen Valley to White Wolf, past Tenaya Lake and through Tuolumne Meadows to Tioga Pass, linking the Big Oak Flat wagon road on the west with the Tioga mining district on the Sierra crest. Construction crews began blasting and grading the roadbed late that year, halted for the winter, and then pushed on furiously in 1883, finishing the work on Sept. 4 of that year.

The road was little used, if at all, by the company that built it, which found little or no valuable ore and suspended Tioga mining operations in 1884, leaving the road to deteriorate. Although the state of California completed an automobile road up Lee Vining Canyon in 1908, linking the east-side settlements and railroads with the older wagon road across the park, the Tioga Road was used by few travelers. Regular maintenance was not performed until the road was acquired by the federal government in 1915 as a potentially valuable tourist route to Yosemite Valley.

The road was subsequently rebuilt, widened and paved. Over the following half-century it was also realigned and rerouted, especially the section west of White Wolf. Portions of the old wagon route have been preserved, however, and motorists who want a taste of the experience that greeted travelers early in this century may sample the rough, narrow, twisting roads to the Yosemite Creek campground, White Wolf and the May Lake trailhead.

In its traverse of Yosemite National Park's high country, the Tioga Road leads past innumerable hiking opportunities. Trails lead from the road to glacier-carved canyons, alpine lakes, tumbling streams, emerald meadows and serrated peaks. From many of them are views of Yosemite Valley and its landmark scenery, the familiar shapes given new aspect by the altered perspective.

The hikes in this section sample all these things, in trips ranging from easy hour-long jaunts to strenuous all-day ascents. All begin at fairly high elevations, some rising above 10,000 feet, so it is a good idea to spend a day or two in the area to become acclimated before hitting the trail. Prepare also for rapidly changing weather; this near the Sierra crest, afternoon thunderstorms are common and it's no fun to be caught in a downpour of rain or hail without waterproof clothing. On trails that cross exposed ridgetops it's best to turn back when a storm threatens, as the cliffs and domes are frequent targets of lightning.   ■

Tuolumne Meadows from Lembert Dome

Hike #31: Cascade Creek

Distance	4 miles
Level of difficulty	Easy
Child rating	5 and up
Starting elevation	6360 feet
Lowest point on trail	6000 feet
Topographic maps	Tamarack Flat, El Capitan 7.5';
	Hetch Hetchy Reservoir, Yosemite 15'
Guidebook map	19

This easy hike to lovely Cascade Creek is a good one if you are staying at Tamarack Flat Campground, which is about 3 miles down a lousy, potholed road from Tioga Road 3¾ miles east of Crane Flat.

The trailhead is at the south end of the campground, where the main campground road reaches a locked gate. Your route lies along an abandoned road—the original Big Oak Flat Road, which once extended from a mining town 30 miles west of the present-day park boundary, through Tamarack Flat, and descended all the way to the floor of Yosemite Valley, which it reached near the foot of El Capitan. It was the second road built into the valley, completed in 1874, and was used by automobiles until 1945 when huge landslides blocked the steep switchbacks on the talus slopes above the valley floor.

Following the landslides, traffic was switched to the current Big Oak Flat Road, completed in 1940, and the old road was abandoned. It now serves only hikers, but its line of descent along the north wall of Yosemite Valley is still visible from the south side of the valley.

Tamarack Flat takes its name from an old term for the lodgepole pines so common in the area. The trail passes through a stand of these trees, soon intermixed with Jeffrey pines, incense cedars, white firs and sugar pines, as it heads downhill from the campground, passing through fire-scarred areas that support sprays of blue penstemon and paintbrush.

At 1.4 miles the route crosses a small tributary of Cascade Creek, which passes through a culvert beneath the road. Along the creek's banks here are plentiful ferns, willows, umbrella plants, azaleas and serviceberries. The road descends more steeply from here, following the course of the creek. It passes a junction with a trail to the new Big Oak Flat Road at 1.6 miles, and reaches a bridge across boulder-strewn Cascade Creek at 2 miles.

The creek descends steeply in a series of small pools and cascades—whence the name—and makes a delightful picnic spot.

Return the way you came.   ■

Hike #32: Cathedral Lake

Distance	7 miles
Level of difficulty	Moderate
Child rating	10 and up
Starting elevation	8560 feet
Highest point on trail	9560 feet
Topographic maps	Tenaya Lake 7.5';
	Tuolumne Meadows 15'
Guidebook map	20

Lying in the shadow of craggy Cathedral Peak, the twin Cathedral Lakes reward a long ascent with classic subalpine scenery. This hike leads to the larger and lower of the two lakes, a popular destination for backpackers, who crowd its shores on weekends. It's not a difficult day hike, however, and is probably better enjoyed that way.

The trailhead is at the Cathedral Lakes parking area, which is identified by a sign on the south side of the Tioga Road just 1.5 miles west of the Tuolumne Meadows campground entrance.

The trail starts next to Budd Creek, reaches a junction at 0.1 mile (continue straight ahead) and immediately leads uphill, climbing nearly 600 feet over the first ¾ mile. The trail is often dusty, testimony to the heavy use it receives, as it passes through a forest of lodgepole pine. As you gain elevation, you'll notice red fir, white fir, whitebark pine and sugar pines joining the forest.

The trail levels at 0.7 mile and then undulates gently for the next half a mile, passing the base of Cathedral Peak—the actual summit is not visible yet—and crossing a small creek at 1.4 miles. Climbing steeply now, the trail reaches a spring at 1.5 miles, a spot that provides a good view northward to Fairview Dome.

At 1.7 miles the trail levels off and enters a stand of whitebark pine. Whitebarks and lodgepoles look much alike, both having bark like small jigsaw-puzzle pieces. But as a whitebark grows older and larger, the bark on its upper trunk and branches grows much paler than the bark on the dark gray lodgepole trunks.

At 2.2 miles the trail begins descending, and the spires atop Cathedral Peak come into view overhead to the left. Ahead lies the angular mass of Tresidder Peak, named after Donald Tresidder, a former president of Stanford University who headed the Yosemite Park & Curry Co. from 1925 to1948, when it built the Ahwahnee Hotel and the string of High Sierra camps.

At 3 miles the trail splits, the left fork leading to upper Cathedral Lake and over Cathedral Pass. Bear right and descend along the course of a small creek to the marshy meadows at the east end of Lower Cathedral Lake, which we reach at 3.5 miles.

Behind you rises Cathedral Peak, carved into sharp horns by the gnawing of glaciers at its flanks. The lake is rimmed by bedrock, which bears the telltale grooves and scratches produced by moving rivers of ice. Erratics—boulders carried by the ice and deposited when the glacier melted—dot the area, which offers good views across Tenaya Canyon to Polly Dome and Pywiack Dome above the shores of Tenaya Lake.

Return the way you came.   ■

Cathedral Peak and Lower Cathedral Lake

National Park Service

Hike #33: Dog Lake

Distance	2.4 miles
Level of difficulty	Easy
Child rating	5 and up
Starting elevation	8600 feet
Highest point on trail	9170 feet
Topographic maps	Tioga Pass 7.5';
	Tuolumne Meadows 15'
Guidebook map	20

Dog Lake is easy to reach from the Tuolumne Meadows area, and is a popular picnic destination for dayhikers. Fortunately it is large enough to offer solitude even on a busy summer weekend, its long shoreline providing plenty of shady spots to take in the view.

The trailhead is at the Lembert Dome parking area, on the north side of the Tioga Road at the east end of Tuolumne Meadows. The trail leads north out of the parking area, crossing a sandy flat and forking at 0.1 mile. The right fork leads up Lembert Dome (Hike #37), so we stay to the left, gaining elevation and passing two junctions with trails leading to Tuolumne Stables, where horseback rides can be arranged. Take the right fork each time.

The trail begins climbing more steeply at 0.3 mile, passing through lodgepole-pine forest. At 0.6 mile it steepens again, before reaching a more open, damp and grassy area punctuated by the yellow spires of arrowhead groundsel and the rounded, pinkish flowers of swamp onions.

The trail continues to climb, more gently now, reaching a junction at 0.8 mile with the trail to the Dog Lake parking area to the right. Continue on the left, passing another junction at 1 mile, this time with the Young Lakes trail. Bear right, reaching the shore of the lake at 1.2 mile.

Dog Lake was named by Robert Marshall of the U.S. Geological Survey in 1898 because he found an abandoned sheepdog here with a litter of puppies. The lake is broad and shallow, offering pleasant wading and swimming. To the east, the reddish-brown peaks of Mts. Dana, Gibbs and Lewis, left to right, provide a colorful and contrasting backdrop to the sky-blue lake.

Return the way you came. ∎

Hike #34: Elizabeth Lake

Distance	4.4 miles
Level of difficulty	Moderate
Child rating	10 and up
Starting elevation	8680 feet
Highest point on trail	9487 feet
Topographic maps	Vogelsang Peak 7.5';
	Tuolumne Meadows 15'
Guidebook map	20

Nestled beneath the craggy spire of Unicorn Peak, beautiful Elizabeth Lake is a popular destination for hikers staying in the Tuolumne Meadows campground, so you'll likely find yourself sharing it with other visitors. Although not long, the hike involves a steady climb of about 800 feet, which is likely to make younger children balk.

The trail starts in the campground, adjacent to the restrooms near the group area. If you aren't staying in the campground, drive in and stop at the entrance kiosk for a parking pass and a campground map, which will direct you to the trailhead.

The trail crosses the John Muir Trail after about 50 yards, and then climbs steeply through a pure stand of lodgepole pine, crossing a small stream at 0.5 mile and another at 1 mile, the latter lined by red-flowering mountain heather. The climb grows less steep past this point, and at 1.1 miles you begin hearing the song of Unicorn Creek in the distance to the right.

At 1.2 miles the trail is nearly level, as it passes a small brook and reaches a grassy area dotted with small lodgepole pines. Ahead you can see the distinctive pointed spire of Unicorn Peak, one of the summits in the Cathedral Range, which extends northwest-southeast across this corner of the park.

The trail reaches the side of Unicorn Creek at 1.6 miles and follows it toward the lake. From the forks at 1.7 miles both paths lead to the lake, but the one to the left also brings you to a lovely meadow crossed by the meandering creek and is preferable. Taking that branch, we walk another tenth of a mile before reaching another fork in the trail; this time we turn right, crossing the creek and reaching the lake at 2.2 miles.

The views from the lake are spectacular, including the craggy Cathedral Range to the south and southeast, as well as the distant, snowy summits north of Tuolumne Meadows along the Sierra crest. The lakeshore is marshy in places, but by strolling around it you can find plenty of scenic spots suitable for picnicking.

Return the way you came.   ■

Hike #35: Gaylor Lakes

Distance	3 miles
Level of difficulty	Strenuous
Child rating	10 and up
Starting elevation	9960 feet
Highest point on trail	10760 feet
Topographic maps	Tioga Pass 7.5';
	Tuolumne Meadows, Mono Craters 15'
Guidebook map	23

In a way the trail to Gaylor Lakes is the climax of all the hikes along the Tioga Road, for it leads to the Great Sierra Mine—the reason the forerunner of the Tioga Road was built. Along the way it climbs into a treeless land of barren rock, past sparkling blue lakes of icy clarity, into a region where the air is thin and the views of craggy, snow-capped peaks seem to go on forever. It's the soul of the Sierra revealed, stripped of distractions, reduced to the essentials: rock, water, sky.

The trailhead is adjacent to the Tioga Pass park entrance, in a small parking lot on the west side of the road. There's a restroom here, but no water.

The trail heads due west, climbing very steeply—so steeply, that even if you've wisely taken the time to grow accustomed to the high elevation, you'll have to pause repeatedly to catch your breath. The good things about the climb are that it doesn't last long, and that awe-inspiring views begin unfolding almost immediately to the east, where Mt. Dana and the Kuna Crest rear high above the small meadows alongside the road.

Now the trail passes through lodgepole and whitebark pine, switchbacking several times before leaving the forest behind and crossing bare rock to a saddle at 0.4 mile. The view expands here to include the Sierra Crest to the north and the Cathedral Range to the southeast.

The trail switchbacks down a steep, dusty slope to the shore of Middle Gaylor Lake at 0.6 mile. At the lakeshore, bear right, following the trail around to the lake's north end. Just after you cross the lake's inlet, take the trail fork that veers off to the right, proceeding almost due north across a boulder-strewn plateau devoid of trees.

Climbing slightly, the trail passes the base of reddish-brown Gaylor Peak before reaching the shore of upper Gaylor Lake. Keep to the left along the shoreline, crossing colorful rock outcroppings and following the trail up a steep slope at the lake's north end. At 1.4 miles the trail reaches a stone cabin perched on the lip of the ridge. Built entirely of native rock, without benefit of mortar, it is remarkably well-preserved considering the ferocity of winter conditions in this lonely, exposed site more than 10,000 feet above sea level.

The trail continues past the cabin and then peters out in the vicinity of the Great Sierra Mine, at 1.5 miles. Numerous open shafts, fragments of equipment and crumbling wooden frameworks dot the area, which was bustling with activity in 1881. The Great Sierra Mining Co. began work that year on its main tunnel, which extended 1,784 feet into the mountain but never struck the rich silver vein prospectors believed ran beneath Tioga hill. This is the site of the "city" of Dana, which was given its own post office in 1880 but ceased to exist four years later.

More than 16,000 pounds of machinery was hauled up the sheer eastern scarp to this location by the mining company, and miners swarmed to the area. Just to the north they established the town of Bennettville, where the Great Sierra Mining Co. made its headquarters.

Few of the mines in the entire district ever struck pay dirt, and the Great Sierra mine was one of the utter failures. Although the company built the Great Sierra Wagon Road to link its mines with the railroads on the west side of the mountains, it went out of business in 1884—shortly after the road was completed. Dana and Bennettville became ghost towns

Be careful when exploring the area around the mines, especially if you have children with you. The shafts are not fenced off, and should not be entered. Some of the mining equipment has been removed to Wawona, where it is on display at the Pioneer History Center.

Return the way you came.   ■

Ruins of Great Sierra Mine Cabin above Gaylor Lakes

Hike #36: Harden Lake

Distance	5 miles
Level of difficulty	Easy
Child rating	10 and up
Starting elevation	7875 feet
Lowest point on trail	7400 feet
Topographic maps	Tamarack Flat, Hetch Hetchy Reservoir 7.5'; Hetch Hetchy Reservoir 15'
Guidebook map	21

Although Harden Lake is a largely uninspiring destination, the hike to it follows the course of the lovely, tumbling Middle Fork Tuolumne River most of the way. As a bonus, the trail follows a remnant of the original Great Sierra Wagon Road, forerunner of today's Tioga Road, offering hikers a chance to imagine the challenges facing travelers in the nineteenth century.

The trail begins at White Wolf, where there's a lodge offering meals, cabin rentals and a small store. The Park Service also maintains employee housing here, and there's an 87-site campground.

Park near the lodge, and walk downhill on the road past the campground entrance, continuing beyond the point where the road is closed to traffic. The road crosses the river and heads downhill, paralleling the stream for the next mile. It then heads away from the water, after passing a spur road to the left that leads to a sewage treatment pond. The road levels briefly before starting downhill again and reaching a trail junction at 1.6 miles. Stay left, keeping to the road.

At 1.7 miles, aspen trees appear along the road, joining a forest that includes ponderosa, lodgepole and sugar pines. The road forks at 1.9 miles, the left branch continuing along the route of the original Great Sierra Wagon Road, following the river to Aspen Valley and eventually reaching the park boundary north of the Big Oak Flat entrance.

We bear right at the junction and climb about 80 feet over the next 0.1 mile. The road then levels off and at 2.2 miles leads through a marshy area filled with corn lilies, lupine, sneezeweed and bluebells. At 2.3 miles we reach a junction. Bear right to reach the shore of the small lake at 2.5 miles.

Harden Lake is really just a boulder-filled depression, accumulating runoff from the surrounding area but having no real outlet or inlet streams. As a result, it shrinks throughout the summer and is best visited early in the season, when the shallow, sun-warmed water makes for good swimming and wading.

Return the way you came.   ■

Hike #37: Lembert Dome

Distance	2 miles
Level of difficulty	Moderate
Child rating	10 and up
Starting elevation	8600 feet
Highest point on trail	9450 feet
Topographic maps	Tioga Pass 7.5';
	Tuolumne Meadows 15'
Guidebook map	20

Although steep, the trail up Lembert Dome is short and leads to the best view of Tuolumne Meadows and the surrounding area. The dome is a giant *roche moutonée,* a French term meaning "rock sheep" that is used to designate a glacier-sculpted formation characterized by sloping back and sheer front. One is produced when a glacier flows over a resistant mass of bedrock, polishing the uphill side as it climbs up and over the mass, and then chiseling off the downhill face, snagging the rock and quarrying it away along natural joints.

Lembert Dome was named for Jean Baptiste Lembert, a sheepherder and amateur naturalist who homesteaded in Tuolumne Meadows in 1885. He summered there in a cabin he built, collecting plants, butterflies and other insects, until 1896, when he was found shot to death in his cabin. The killing was never solved.

The trail to the top of the dome begins at the Lembert Dome parking area, on the north side of the Tioga Road at the east end of Tuolumne Meadows. It leads north, reaching a junction at 0.1 mile. The left branch leads to Dog Lake, described in Hike #33. Turn right, beginning a steep climb through lodgepole-pine forest along the west flank of the dome.

The climb is strenuous but doesn't last long, reaching a saddle at 0.7 mile. From here, a faint track leads to your right onto the back of the dome, which slopes steeply away east and west. The trail quickly disappears on the bare rock, but it is not difficult to pick a route south toward the summit, reached at 1 mile.

The views are fantastic, taking in the meadows below as well as the peaks of the Cathedral Range to the south. The walk out to the summit is unnerving, however, and not advised for those afraid of heights or accompanied by children. Views that are nearly as satisfactory may be obtained, however, by walking only 50 yards or so onto the exposed back of the dome, stopping before the drop grows too steep for comfort.

Return the way you came.   ■

Hike #38: Lukens Lake

Distance	1.6 miles
Level of difficulty	Easy
Child rating	5 and up
Starting elevation	8180 feet
Highest point on trail	8340 feet
Topographic maps	Yosemite Falls 7.5';
	Hetch Hetchy Reservoir 15'
Guidebook map	22

An easy hike leads to this small lake, popular with anglers. It's a pleasant picnic spot and a good destination if you have young children, especially if you have only recently arrived in the high country along the Tioga Road and are not yet used to the elevation.

The trailhead is on the north side of the road, across from a signed turnout on the Tioga Road about 16 miles east of Crane Flat. No water or restrooms are available here.

The broad trail leads through a dense stand of red fir, a beautiful tree common along the Tioga Road, which grows best on deep. well-drained soils in the zone that receives the heaviest Sierran snowfall. Their deeply furrowed, red-brown bark is often decorated by bright chartreuse blotches of staghorn lichen, and you can tell the upper limit of the winter snowpack by the lower limit of the lichen's growth.

The trail heads uphill on a moderate incline toward a saddle, which it reaches at 0.2 mile. Shattered fragments of trees litter the ground here, a common sight in red-fir forests. Because of their great height—which can reach 180 feet—and the fact they grow in the area that receives the most thunderstorm activity, they are often the targets of lightning.

From the saddle, the trail descends steadily toward the lake, crossing a feeder stream at 0.5 mile. The moist area is blanketed by mountain bluebell, shooting star, corn lily, and the odd-shaped blooms of elephant heads, tiny pink flowers that look like upraised elephant trunks.

Beyond the stream the trail crosses a moist meadow at the southeast end of the lake. Trees are invading the meadow, which is in turn gradually replacing the lake as it fills with sediment. The trail curves around the lakeshore to the northeast, reaching pleasant forest-shaded picnic spots at 0.8 mile.

Return the way you came.   ■

Hike #39: May Lake

Distance	2.2 miles
Level of difficulty	Moderate
Child rating	5 and up
Starting elevation	8846 feet
Highest point on trail	9329 feet
Topographic maps	Tenaya Lake 7.5';
	Tuolumne Meadows 15'
Guidebook map	25

May Lake is a gem, nestled beneath the rocky, multi-crested hump of Mt. Hoffmann and ringed by pines, hemlock and mountain heather. It is also the site of one of the park's five High Sierra camps, situated a day's hike apart, where food and lodging in tent cabins may be arranged in advance for a price. Together the camps and their connecting trails form the High Sierra Loop, a 50-mile circuit of the backcountry surrounding Tuolumne Meadows.

The trail to May Lake begins at the end of a 1.8-mile paved road that heads north from the Tioga Road about 4 miles west of Tenaya Lake. The narrow road leading to the trailhead is a remnant of the original Great Sierra Wagon Road, forerunner of the Tioga Road, built in 1882-1883 to link the communities west of the present-day park boundaries with mining prospects at Tioga Pass.

The trail begins on the north side of the parking area. No water or restrooms are available. Heading across a sandy flat, the trail passes beneath red and white fir and lodgepole pine, and then begins a moderate climb.

At 0.4 mile the trees thin as the trail passes into a rocky bowl and continues its climb. At 0.5 mile views begin to open up eastward across Tenaya Canyon. As the trail continues to gain elevation, the views expand until you can turn around and look back to the south at the rounded hump of Half Dome and the great granite sweep of Clouds Rest. In the distance to the southeast rises the distinctive spire of Mt. Clark.

At 0.8 mile the trail levels briefly and provides breathtaking views to the east, where the gleaming spires of the Cathedral Range wear their coats of snow and ice even in midsummer. The trail then resumes its climb and reaches May Lake at 1.1 miles. A backpackers' camping area lies to the left, while the tent cabins and facilities of May Lake High Sierra Camp lie to the right.

Across the lake rises Mt. Hoffmann, 10,850 feet, which was tall enough to protrude above the massive glacier that carved out Tenaya Canyon. Named after Charles F. Hoffmann, principal topographer of the California State Geological Survey led by Josiah Whitney in 1863, Mt. Hoffmann marks the approximate geographical center of Yosemite National Park.

Return the way you came. ■

Hike #40: Mono Pass

Distance	7.6 miles
Level of difficulty	Strenuous
Child rating	10 and up
Starting elevation	9680 feet
Highest point on trail	10604 feet
Topographic maps	Tioga Pass, Mount Dana, Koip Peak 7.5'; Tuolumne Meadows, Mono Craters 15'
Guidebook map	23

The beauty of the Sierra Nevada reaches its most austere in the alpine zone, where trees are absent, the flowers keep their heads low to escape the wind, and bare stone dominates the landscape. It is a region at once forbidding and exhilarating, a place where hiking is difficult because of the steepness and the diminished oxygen, but rewarding because of the generally spectacular views.

Mono Pass lies on the eastern boundary of Yosemite National Park, on the Sierra crest. It is in an area where the pale granite backbone of the mountain range gives way to the reds, browns and blacks of metamorphic rock, ancient deposits changed by the heat of magma welling up from deep in the earth. Such zones often contain valuable minerals, and the Mono Pass region is dotted by old mine shafts, weathered log cabins and other evidence of the search for wealth during the late 19th century.

The trail begins in Dana Meadows, at a pullout 1.5 miles south of the Tioga Pass park entrance, marked by a sign "Mono Pass." No water or restrooms are available.

The trail leads southeast from the parking area, descending to cross the meadows, which are flanked by Mammoth Peak to the south and Mts. Gibbs and Dana to the east. At 0.3 mile it crosses the Dana Fork Tuolumne River, an easy boulder-hopping ford, where blue lupine, flame-colored paintbrush, daisies and lacy white yampah enliven the scenery. The trail then climbs over a series of moraines, low ridges composed of debris scraped together by the great Tuolumne glacier. It was born among these peaks and flowed to the west along the course of the Tuolumne River, eventually extending more than 60 miles to its terminus in the foothills

At 1.1 miles the trail, continuing its moderate climb, reaches the collapsing remnants of a log cabin, one of many built in the area in the 1880s during the brief and ultimately fruitless mining boom.

Beyond the cabin the trail, now passing through stands of whitebark pine, nears the bank of Parker Pass Creek, which winds picturesquely through meadows at the base of Mammoth Peak. At 1.3 miles the trail crosses the path of an avalanche, which carved an obvious scar through the forest on the side of Mt. Gibbs, to your left.

The trail then enters an open area dotted by aromatic sagebrush and inhabited by dozens of Belding ground squirrels, which pop up from their burrows and stand erect like little sentries to watch you pass. At 2.3 miles the trail reaches a junction with the Spillway Lake trail (Hike #42). Go left to begin a steeper climb that takes you away from the creek and back into the forest, reaching the ruins of another cabin at 3.1 miles.

As you gain elevation, the whitebark pines become shorter and wider, an adaptation to the bitter cold and biting winds that rake the area in winter. At 3.5 miles the trail forks, the spur on the right leading 0.3 mile to a cluster of six well-preserved log cabins on a low ridge near an abandoned mine shaft. The cabins are worth a side trip, standing in mute testimony to the life of hardship and solitude that greeted 19th century prospectors in their search for silver and gold. Be careful, however, especially if you have children with you: The abandoned mine shaft, filled with foul-smelling water, is unprotected and dangerous.

To reach Mono Pass bear left at this junction, arriving at the summit at 3.8 miles. A small lake straddles the pass, which also marks the national-park boundary. The sign says the elevation is 10,599 feet, but more recent maps put it at 10,604. For spectacular views, continue along the trail less than ½ mile to the top of Bloody Canyon, a great gash in the eastern face of the Sierra Nevada. From here it is possible to look east to Mono Lake and beyond to the Wassuk, Excelsior and White mountains along the Nevada border.

Return the way you came.   ■

Old miners' cabins at Mono Pass

Hike #41: North Dome

Distance	9.8 miles
Level of difficulty	Moderate
Child rating	10 and up
Starting elevation	8120 feet
Highest point on trail	8522 feet
Topographic maps	Yosemite Falls 7.5';
	Hetch Hetchy Reservoir 15'
Guidebook map	24

The view from broad North Dome is perhaps the best of any along the rim of Yosemite Valley, a spectacular panorama of naked stone and ice-carved peaks. Located above the northeast end of the valley, North Dome offers a unique perspective on Half Dome, which lies seemingly close enough to touch, as well as on Cloud's Rest, a 4000-foot sweep of polished stone rising above Tenaya Canyon. As a bonus, the trail leads past Indian Rock, a rare, natural stone arch on top of Indian Ridge.

The trailhead is at a pullout on the south side of Tioga Road, marked with a sign identifying it as Porcupine Creek. The spot marks the entrance to the old Porcupine Creek campground, now closed, 1 mile east of the entrance to present-day Porcupine Flat Campground.

Follow the abandoned road downhill to the former campground, at 0.5 mile, where the trail begins on the bank of a small tributary of Porcupine Creek. Cross the stream, which supports a garden of daisies, lupine, yampah and corn lilies, heading south through a lodgepole-pine forest to a crossing of Porcupine Creek only a hundred yards beyond.

Porcupine Flat and creek take their names from a common inhabitant of the area, the second-largest North American rodent. Porcupines feed on the inner bark of conifers, especially lodgepole pines, and are members of a class of rodents that includes the guinea pig, chinchilla, nutria and capybara of South America. You can tell they've been around by the bare, gnawed spots they leave on trees where they've fed.

The trail undulates through the forest, crossing another small creek at 0.9 mile. At 1.5 miles the trail climbs a small rise, reaching a junction at 1.7 miles with the trail to Snow Creek. Take the right fork, walk about 20 yards and then turn left at the next junction.

The trail contours briefly along the side of Indian Ridge before climbing a short distance, emerging onto a fairly open slope at 2 miles, where views of Yosemite Valley appear. After leveling briefly, the trail resumes its climb, switchbacking up a moderately steep incline and reaching a saddle at 2.8 miles. A spur trail leads from here 0.25 mile to the natural arch atop Indian Rock, a worthwhile digression. (The spur climbs steeply up a rocky slope, reaching the top of the ridge and following it north to the arch, a small but unusual feature. The only other known natural arch in Yosemite National Park is underwater in the Dana Fork Tuolumne River, in Tuolumne Meadows. Indian Rock is a good vantage point, offering views of Half Dome, the Clark Range and—on a very clear day—the Coast Ranges to the west.)

Return to the main trail at 3.3 miles and turn left, continuing southwest for a mile along the crest of Indian Ridge through a forest of scattered red firs, which give way to Jeffrey pines as the trail descends.

The trail reaches a junction at 4.5 miles with the path to Yosemite Falls. Bear left, beginning a short series of switchbacks down a steep slope at 4.6 miles. The trail levels out at the bottom of the slope and then climbs gently onto the broad back of North Dome, reaching the top at 4.9 miles.

Plan on spending some time here, because the views are breathtaking. Half Dome looms up, seemingly within arm's length, just to the southeast, while the great, gleaming sweep of naked stone that is Clouds Rest stands guard over Tenaya Canyon to the east-northeast. From the edge of North Dome, you can see into Yosemite Valley, and watch sunlight glinting off the windshields of cars as they creep down the road to Glacier Point, directly across the valley to the south. Below and to the left of Glacier Point is wispy Illilouette Fall; above and to the right of the point is the bald crown of Sentinel Dome (Hike #47).

Return the way you came.						■

Hike #42: Spillway Lake

Distance	7.4 miles
Level of difficulty	Strenuous
Child rating	10 and up
Starting elevation	9680 feet
Highest point on trail	10450 feet
Topographic maps	Tioga Pass, Mount Dana, Koip Peak 7.5'; Tuolumne Meadows, Mono Craters 15'
Guidebook map	23

Located at the foot of the Kuna Crest, Spillway Lake is an out-of-the-way destination offering solitude among the clouds. The trailhead is the same as for Hike #40, the Mono Pass trail, and follows the same route for the first 2.3 miles.

At the signed junction where the Mono Pass and Spillway Lake trails diverge, bear right, following Parker Pass Creek through a series of meadows strewn with flowers, including lupine, gentian, paintbrush, yampah and larkspur. At 2.4 miles the trail briefly re-enters the forest, quickly returning to sagebrush and then meadow again.

Climbing moderately, the trail reaches the end of the meadow at 3.1 miles and heads for the bank of the creek, which it follows upstream through a stand of small willows. At 3.4 miles the trees are left behind, and the trail crosses an open expanse dotted with boulders and covered with short, wiry grasses and sedges.

Soon the trail grows faint and then disappears, but the small lake is in sight directly ahead. Cross the meadow, being careful not to crush the delicate plant life, to the reach the shore at 3.7 miles.

Return the way you came.   ∎

Hike #43: Sunrise Lakes

Distance	5.4 miles
Level of difficulty	Moderate
Child rating	10 and up
Starting elevation	8150 feet
Highest point on trail	9166 feet
Topographic maps	Tenaya Lake 7.5';
	Tuolumne Meadows 15'
Guidebook map	25

A steep climb up the side of Tenaya Canyon is rewarded on this hike by expansive views of glacier-carved peaks and a picturesque picnic spot on the shore of one of the Sunrise Lakes.

The trailhead is in the former walk-in campground at the southwest end of Tenaya Lake. The popular campground has been closed to let the damaged wetlands along the lake shore recover from the impact of visitors. Park either in the pullout across the road from the gated campground entrance or at the signed Sunrise Lakes parking lot just to the west.

Follow the road east through the campground to the edge of a small meadow and pick up the trail that heads to the left. Follow it across the small outlet stream from the lake, and then bear right at a junction a few yards from the creek. Here the broad, level trail enters dense lodgepole-pine forest, and follows the course of the creek.

At 0.2 mile the trail reaches a junction with a trail to Tuolumne Meadows. Bear right, continuing along a level course for another 0.4 mile. At 0.6 mile the trail begins climbing, crossing a small creek at 0.8 miles and beginning to offer views back down into Tenaya Canyon. The trail crosses two more small creeks and then steepens at 1.6 miles as the ascent out of the canyon begins in earnest.

Over the next ½ mile, the trail switchbacks up a steep slope, gaining 800 feet in elevation. With each step, however, the view to the north grows more spectacular, encompassing Mt. Hoffman, Tuolumne Peak and the other ice-polished granite walls above Tenaya Canyon. The deep canyon was carved by a branch of the huge Tuolumne glacier, and the naked stone gleams in the sunlight.

The trail tops out at 2.2 miles, at a fork on a sparsely forested saddle. Take the left fork, which drops gently downhill another ½ mile to the shore of Lower Sunrise Lake, a good picnic spot, at 2.7 miles. This small lake lies at the base of a steep, rocky slope, which presents good examples of exfoliation—the process by which exposed bodies of granite crack and shed layers of stone.

Beyond the lake the trail climbs past middle and upper Sunrise Lakes, and eventually leads to the Sunrise High Sierra Camp.

Return the way you came.   ■

Hike #44: Tenaya Lake

Distance	2.2 miles
Level of difficulty	Easy
Child rating	5 and up
Starting elevation	8150 feet
Highest point on trail	8200 feet
Topographic maps	Tenaya Lake 7.5';
	Tuolumne Meadows 15'
Guidebook map	25

Set in its gleaming granite basin, Tenaya Lake is one of the most beautiful bodies of water in the Sierra Nevada, rivaling even Lake Tahoe. Good views of Tenaya Lake, named after the last leader of Yosemite Valley's Ahwahneeche tribe, are provided at Olmsted Point on the Tioga Road, but it's easy to stroll around the lake and appreciate it from a more intimate perspective.

The trailhead is in the old walk-in campground at the southwest end of the lake. The campground is closed now, and parking is available near the gated campground entrance or just to the west at the Sunrise Lakes parking lot.

Follow the old campground road east and pick up the trail at the edge of a small meadow near the lake's outlet. Cross the outlet stream, and then bear left at the junction, heading for the lakeshore. When you reach it, stay to the right through the abandoned campsites and pick up the well-defined trail just uphill from the water.

The trail leads along the lake's east shore, climbing about 50 feet above the water as it passes through a forest of sugar and lodgepole pines. Across the lake to the north rises massive Polly Dome, while smaller Pywiack Dome looms to the northeast. "Pywiack," the name the local Indians gave Tenaya Lake, means "the place of shining rocks," a reference to the glacial polish on the surrounding cliffs that reflects the sunlight like a mirror under the right conditions.

At the lake's northeast end, the trail forks at 1 mile, the right branch leading all the way to Tuolumne Meadows. Turn left, skirting the sandy beach and the picnic area, and crossing a series of small inlet streams. A strong up-canyon breeze keeps the beach here rather chilly, and provides sport for windsurfers willing to brave the lake's chilly waters.

On the north side of the lake, reached at 1.3 miles, your route lies on pavement, paralleling Tioga Road along the shoulder for nearly half a mile until you reach another picnic area, where you can cut in toward the shore again. While walking next to the traffic is not particularly enjoyable, you can use the time to watch climbers making their spiderlike way up the steeply sloping face of Polly Dome.

At the picnic area, at 1.7 miles, the trail veers from the road and takes you through an increasingly dense stand of lodgepole pines. When you get tired of fighting with them, you can try the shoulder of the road again as it curves around the lake, and follow it back to your car at 2.2 miles.   ■

Tenaya Lake and the domes above it

Hike #45: Tuolumne Falls

Distance	8.2 miles
Level of difficulty	Moderate
Child rating	10 and up
Starting elevation	8600 feet
Lowest point on trail	8120 feet
Topographic maps	Tioga Pass, Falls Ridge 7.5';
	Tuolumne Meadows 15'
Guidebook map	20

Waterfall connoisseurs can easily become spoiled in Yosemite National Park, thanks to the peerless fountains of spray and mist decorating the walls of Yosemite Valley. Compared to those leaping torrents, the far more restrained Tuolumne Falls—really only a large cascade—would seem to hardly merit mention. But the trail to it constitutes one of the classic walks in the Yosemite high country, following a section of the justly famous Pacific Crest Trail as it skirts Tuolumne Meadows and then follows the crystalline Tuolumne River into its deepening gorge.

To reach the trailhead, turn off the Tioga Road at the sign indicating the Lembert Dome parking area, at the east end of Tuolumne Meadows. Either park in the lot at the base of the dome, or drive down the dirt road ⅓ mile to a locked gate and park near it. The trail begins at the gate, where a sign indicates the start of the Glen Aulin Trail.

Past the gate, hike along the road, a remnant of the original Tioga wagon road, as it skirts the meadow. To the south, the spires of Unicorn Peak and Cathedral Peak jut into the sky, providing a majestic backdrop to the meadow and its meandering river. Keep an eye out for little Belding ground squirrels, which pop out of the grass and sit upright on their haunches to watch as you pass their many burrows.

At 0.4 mile the road forks; bear right, reaching a trail about 50 yards farther. Follow it to Soda Springs, naturally effervescent mineral springs that bubble from the ground, and past Parsons Lodge, built in 1915 by the Sierra Club and later deeded to the Park Service for use as an interpretive center.

The trail turns rocky after it passes the lodge and enters a lodgepole-pine forest where it begins a gentle descent that will continue most of the way to the falls. At 1.1 miles it reaches a junction, our path lying straight ahead. After crossing the branches of Delaney Creek, the trail reaches a junction at 1.4 miles with the trail to Young Lakes. Bear left here, cross expanses of exposed granite and hop over Dingley Creek before reaching the bank of the Tuolumne River at 2.4 miles.

The river is beautiful here, sliding across polished slabs of glistening stone and tumbling in a series of cascades as its channel steepens. The trail contours along the canyon wall, and passes along the base of a cliff at 3.2 miles. Directly across the river is a brownish-black plug of basalt known as Little Devil's Postpile. Like its larger namesake near Mammoth Mountain, it is a column of volcanic rock fractured into geometric shapes along the joints formed as the molten rock cooled.

The trail bends around the cliff, offering tremendous views down the river canyon before descending on a series of rock stairs, re-entering the forest and crossing the Tuolumne River on a bridge at 3.4 miles. As you cross the river and follow it downstream, views open up to the north and northeast, revealing the summits of Mt. Conness and, to its left, Matterhorn Peak.

The trail continues downhill another 0.7 mile to Tuolumne Falls, at 4.1 miles. There are ample boulders and polished slabs of stone at the river's edge in this area, making it a fine place to picnic and sunbathe.

Return the way you came.   ■

The Tuolumne River above Tuolumne Falls

Thomas Winnett

Grizzly Giant

Trails of Wawona and the Glacier Point Road

Approaching Yosemite from the south, visitors follow Highway 41 from Fresno through the foothills, green and flower-strewn in spring, sere and brown in summer, climbing into the forest belt and reaching the park boundary near the Mariposa Grove of giant sequoias. A few miles beyond lies Wawona, its name believed derived from the Native American term for the big trees—"woh-woh-nau"—an imitation of the call of the owl, which served as the sequoias' guardian spirit.

With a campground, a ranger station, the Pioneer History Center, a store and the historic Wawona Hotel, the area is a popular stopping point. It served as headquarters for the Army when it administered Yosemite National Park in the early years, although the region was not incorporated into the park until 1932.

The Victorian-style hotel dates from the 1870s, built by Henry, John and Edward Washburn to serve tourists making their arduous way over the primitive stagecoach road that led to Yosemite Valley. The Washburns also built the Wawona Road, which winds through the mountains approximately along the route taken in 1851 by the members of the Mariposa Battalion, who became the first whites to reach Yosemite Valley. The Wawona Road is open year-round, although some of the visitor attractions in Wawona are closed in winter.

The Glacier Point Road, which branches east from the Wawona Road at Chinquapin, follows the path of a wagon road built in 1882 to carry visitors 16 miles to the spectacular views of Yosemite Valley from its rim. The paved road was constructed in 1936, largely along the route of its dirt predecessor, and is closed in winter past the Badger Pass ski area. Elevations along the Glacier Point road range from 6,000 feet to more than 7,000 feet, offering a cool summertime alternative to Wawona and Yosemite Valley, both at about 4,000 feet.

Compared to Yosemite Valley and the high country north of it, there are relatively few hikes from the two roads in the south half of the park. The trails, however, tend to be used less, although they still offer magnificent views, lessons in history, and examples of the forces that created the Yosemite landscape. Hikes described in this section range from short treks to the precipitous edge of Yosemite Valley, to longer excursions through a variety of mountain life zones.

Between hikes, it's worthwhile to stop at the Pioneer History Center in Wawona, where the Park Service has relocated a variety of historic structures from elsewhere in the park and offers interpretive programs in summer.   ■

Hike #46: Bridalveil Creek

Distance	6.6 miles
Level of difficulty	Easy
Child rating	10 and up
Starting elevation	7000 feet
Highest point on trail	7080 feet
Topographic maps	Half Dome 7.5'; Yosemite 15'
Guidebook map	26

The combination of abundant moisture and sunlight, the latter being the result of a recent forest-thinning fire, makes this easy walk a flower-lover's dream. Dozens of varieties line the trail, reaching their colorful peak bloom in late July and early August. The trail is nearly level, and Bridalveil Creek makes a fine picnic spot.

Although rated for 10-year-olds, the hike is easy. If you want to bring a younger child along, consider going only as far as the creek, rather than continuing all the way to Bridalveil Campground. That would cut the distance in half, and still provide plenty of floral scenery.

The trail begins at the Ostrander Lake trailhead, located in a pullout along the Glacier Point Road just 1.3 miles east of the Bridalveil Campground entrance. Ostrander Lake is a popular destination for cross-country skiers in winter and for backpackers in the summer.

The trail leads south from the parking lot into a fire-scarred lodgepole-pine forest. Many of the trees succumbed to the flames, and where they fell shrubs and grasses have sprung up, along with purple larkspur, lupine and yellow spires of arrowhead groundsel. The trail crosses a small tributary of Bridalveil Creek on a wooden bridge at 0.2 mile.

At 0.6 mile the trail reaches a section of forest almost completely destroyed by the fire, which apparently burned hot enough to consume even large trees. The trail skirts a small meadow at 0.8 mile and continues its level route, passing fiery blooms of red-orange paintbrush and clusters of mountain bluebells nodding at the end of long stems.

At 1.1 miles the trail begins a brief ascent, climbing 80 feet over the next tenth of a mile. Immediately the soil grows drier, and the plant mix changes, buckwheat and lupine replacing the moisture-loving bluebells, larkspur and groundsel. The trail splits at 1.4 miles, the left branch leading to Ostrander Lake. Bear right, following the trail downhill to an easy boulder-hopping crossing of Bridalveil Creek at 1.5 miles.

The creek is small but lovely, and it's hard to believe that so little water could produce something as magical as Bridalveil Fall, which is less than 2 miles downstream. The creek is lined with flowers, including the beautiful red colum-bine, its blooms looking like Chinese lanterns, golden brodiaea and mountain daisies. Across the creek the trail climbs a bit before reaching another junction at 1.7 miles. Turn right, northwest, and parallel the creek as it passes through more burned-over forest.

At 2.2 miles the fire zone is left behind, and the trail contours along the hillside through a shady pine forest. The creek soon reaches a small meadow blanketed by wildflowers, where mosquitos likewise abound. At 2.7 miles the meadow ends, and the trail follows the stream bank to Bridalveil Campground at 3.3 miles.

At one time it was possible to make a loop hike out of this route by picking up a road here and following it northeast past the horse packers' camping area, back to the Glacier Point Road, and then hiking alongside the road for ½ mile along an unofficial trail. The Park Service has closed the packers' road, however, and trees killed by the fire have blocked the unofficial trail.

Return the way you came unless you have planned a shuttle involving two cars—one at the trailhead and the other at the campground. Cutting through the campground and walking back to the trailhead along the Glacier Point Road might be tempting because of the mileage it would save, but is not advised because the road has no real shoulder. ■

Hike #47: Sentinel Dome

Distance	2.2 miles
Level of difficulty	Easy
Child rating	5 and up
Starting elevation	7720 feet
Highest point on trail	8122 feet
Topographic maps	Half Dome 7.5'; Yosemite 15'
Guidebook map	27

Glacier Point may provide one of the best-known views of Yosemite Valley, but to enjoy it you'll have to fight for a parking pace and elbow your way through the crowds lining the railing. At Sentinel Dome, however, you'll find even grander views just a short distance away, and without the heavy traffic common at Glacier Point.

The trailhead is at a parking pullout on the Glacier Point Road, 13 miles from the junction with Highway 41 at Chinquapin and about 2 miles from the road's end at Glacier Point. Water and restrooms are not available.

Follow the trail about 50 yards from the parking area and turn right where the trail splits. The trail crosses a small creek over a wooden bridge, and then climbs a bit before contouring along a rocky, open slope dotted with larkspur. Sentinel Dome is visible ahead and to the left.

At 0.4 mile the trail, ascending gently, enters thicker forest and working its way toward the east side of the dome. The forest here is composed of Jeffrey pine, lodgepole pine and white fir, with manzanita and deer brush filling the occasional open areas.

At 0.6 mile the trail joins an old road that formerly allowed visitors to drive to the base of the dome. Closed now to vehicles, it provides a broad avenue for us as we climb through the forest and emerge on exposed stone at the northeast side of the dome.

There is no real trail up the dome itself, but the way up its broad back is obvious and the climbing is easy. On top, the view is breathtaking, a 360° panorama that includes all of Yosemite Valley, part of Tenaya Canyon, Half Dome, Clouds Rest, Mt. Starr King and the craggy peaks of the Clark Range.

Only one Yosemite Valley landmark is higher: Half Dome. Climbing it, however, is a strenuous and even frightening experience, and can be attempted only after a lengthy hike. For the effort, Sentinel Dome provides the best view in the park. The gnarled, windswept Jeffrey pine on its summit was a popular, much-photographed landmark for many years, but it died in the 1970s, a victim of drought and perhaps the excessive attention of visitors who climbed and hung on it, and carved their names into its bark.

Return the way you came.   ■

Hike #48: Taft Point

Distance	2.2 miles
Level of difficulty	Easy
Child rating	5 and up
Starting elevation	7720 feet
Lowest point on trail	7503 feet
Topographic maps	Half Dome 7.5'; Yosemite 15'
Guidebook map	27

Although this hike is rated for 5-year-olds, an important caveat is in order. The walk is easy, but the destination is a promontory at the edge of a sheer cliff marked by deep fissures. Don't bring children on this hike unless you are certain you can control them. A misstep at the fissures or at the edge of Taft Point would have unfortunate results, since the drop into the valley is a vertical ½ mile.

Warnings aside, the view is spectacular, and is gained with little expense in time and energy. The trailhead is the same as for Hike #47 to Sentinel Dome.

From the parking area, follow the trail about 50 yards and turn left. The trail leads southwest, descending gently to cross tiny Sentinel creek at 0.1 mile and then proceeding almost due west. At 0.6 mile the trail reaches a junction with the Pohono Trail, which leads to the right and takes hikers along the rim of Yosemite Valley to Glacier Point. Continuing straight ahead, our route crosses a small, moist drainage lined by corn lilies and contours briefly along the slope before starting a steeper descent across a rocky hillside at 0.8 mile.

At 0.9 mile the trail passes the first of The Fissures, deep clefts in the edge of Profile Cliff. There are no railings around them, even though they cut through the overhanging stone beneath your feet and open straight to the valley floor below. Use extreme caution near them.

The trail passes The Fissures and reaches the railing atop Profile Cliff at 1 mile. From here hikers have breathtaking views of the west end of Yosemite Valley, including El Capitan, Yosemite Falls and the Three Brothers. Although spectacular, the view is not for the faint of heart, as the rail sits at the very edge of the overhang and the sight of 2,500 feet of air beneath your feet is a bit unnerving. Taft Point itself lies a tenth of a mile to the west, and offers even more extensive views north and northeast, including Mt. Hoffman at the geographic center of the park and Mt. Conness on the Sierra crest.

Taft Point offers perhaps the best perspective for appreciating the great size of El Capitan, rising from the floor of Yosemite Valley in a great, unbroken sweep of naked stone. From the trail the massive cliff can be seen in its entirety, and although it is over a mile away, it is somehow even more impressive than when viewed in closeup from the valley floor.

Return the way you came.   ■

Hike #49: Chilnualna Fall

Distance	8 miles
Level of difficulty	Strenuous
Child rating	10 and up
Starting elevation	4200 feet
Highest point on trail	6400 feet
Topographic maps	Wawona, Mariposa Grove 7.5';
	Yosemite 15'
Guidebook map	28

Early in the season, when the high country is locked in snow, the Wawona area at the south end of the park offers one of the few hiking alternatives to Yosemite Valley. This trail, although strenuous, is the best in that area, offering expansive views of the valley of the South Fork Merced River and a delightful picnic spot near the base of sparkling Chilnualna Fall.

The trailhead is at the end of the Chilnualna Falls Road, which meets Highway 41 about ¼ mile northwest of the entrance to the Wawona store, gas station and Pioneer History Center complex. The turnoff is about a mile southeast of the Wawona Campground.

Drive 1.7 miles on Chilnualna Falls Road and park in the dirt lot, indicated by a sign south of the road just before it makes a hairpin turn. No water or restrooms are available at the trailhead.

The trail leads uphill from the lot and skirts the edge of the paved road before reaching the bank of Chilnualna Creek. Then it passes beneath oaks, ponderosa pines and incense-cedars, and ascends a rock staircase next to a series of cascades. About ¼ mile out, the trail heads uphill away from the stream, reaching a junction at 0.3 mile. Bear to the right up the steep, dry slope, which can be hot in the afternoon.

The trail is lined by mountain misery and manzanita, both lovers of sunlight and tolerant of dry soil. Views begin to open up to the west, encompassing the deep, flat-bottomed river valley and the Chowchilla Mountains on the other side. At 0.8 mile the trail, climbing less steeply now, crosses a small creek and enters a shady ponderosa-pine forest.

At 1.4 miles the climb steepens again and the trail grows dusty as it leaves the shade and begins a series of switchbacks. To the southeast are views of Wawona Dome, 6,897 feet elevation, a steep-sided granite protuberance towering over the Wawona area. The switchbacks continue for about a mile and a half, and at 2.8 miles you reach a good view of large cascades on Chilnualna Creek.

At 3 miles the trail levels as it passes through a thicker forest that includes large sugar pines, and then it crosses a rock slope at the base of a sheer cliff. Arrowhead groundsel, blue penstemon, brodiaea and other flowers grow in crevices in the rocks, and the trail here affords grand views into the valley of the South Fork Merced River.

After a final series of switchbacks, the trail crosses a bare outcrop of granite and reaches the lip of a slope above Chilnualna Creek. From here it's an easy scramble down about 20 feet to the edge of the creek, which you reach at 4 miles. Chilnualna Fall—really just the largest in a series of steep cascades—is visible just upstream, and can be approached by following the small creek along its slickly polished stone bed. Near the water flowers abound, including little leopard lilies, shooting stars, sneezeweed and thick stands of western azaleas. This colorful garden makes a great spot for a picnic before you retrace your steps to the trailhead.   ■

Erratics left by melting glacier

Hike #50: Mariposa Grove

Distance	6.3 miles
Level of difficulty	Moderate
Child rating	10 and up
Starting elevation	5600 feet
Highest point on trail	6600 feet
Topographic maps	Mariposa Grove 7.5'; Yosemite 15'
Guidebook map	29

Yosemite National Park contains three of the 75 remaining groves of giant sequoias, the largest living things on the planet, which grow naturally only on the western slope of the Sierra Nevada between 4500 and 8400 feet elevation.

The Tuolumne and Merced groves are located on the west edge of the park, near the Big Oak Flat and Old Big Oak Flat roads. Both are relatively small, especially in comparison to the extensive groves preserved in Sequoia National Park. The Mariposa Grove, however, is large, containing about 500 mature specimens scattered over 250 acres. Situated at the south end of the park near the Wawona visitor complex, it is also penetrated by a network of trails and roads, making it accessible and extremely popular.

Most visitors pay a fee and ride the open-air trams that provide narrated tours of the grove, shuttling along the roads that are now closed to private vehicle traffic. Others hike only as far as some of the better-known, much-photographed trees in the lower part of the grove. If you're willing to walk a bit farther and aren't afraid of some climbing, you can enjoy the grove without the large crowds.

Mariposa Grove is reached by a 2-mile road that leads east from Highway 41 at the south park entrance. Plan your hike for early in the day or take advantage of the free shuttle bus that operates between the grove and Wawona; by afternoon the grove parking lot is generally full, and traffic on the narrow, twisting road is heavy. Park officials report nearly 1.5 million people a year visit the Mariposa Grove.

Descriptive brochures are available at the trailhead, describing many aspects of sequoia ecology. There are many possible routes through the grove, and the placement of signs at most trail junctions should keep you from getting lost. The route described here takes you on a broad circuit encompassing both the lower and upper parts of the grove, and leading past the best-known landmarks.

From the north side of the parking lot follow the trail northeast, past the base of a toppled sequoia that demonstrates convincingly how shallow is the root system of the giant trees. They have no taproot, and although the massive network of roots from a single tree might cover two to four acres, the roots lie only 4 or 5 feet below the surface.

The trail crosses the tram road and then begins climbing. The tree mix is typical of sequoia groves, which are not the dense, single-variety stands conjured by the term "grove." A sequoia grove typically consists of scattered groups of sequoias, interspersed among far more numerous sugar pines, white firs and incense-cedars.

At 0.3 mile the trail recrosses the tram road and passes the Bachelor Tree and the Three Graces; the Bachelor stands alone a short distance from the closely grouped Graces. At 0.7 mile you reach the 200-foot-tall Grizzly Giant, one of the largest trees in the grove. Others are taller, but few achieve its girth: The tree is 30 feet in diameter at its base, and the giant branch about halfway up the trunk is more than 6 feet thick—larger than many of the surrounding trees. The Grizzly Giant's age is estimated at 2,700 years, making it the oldest sequoia in the Mariposa Grove.

Another tenth of a mile brings you to the California Tree, which has a tunnel cut through it. Such tunnels were popular in the last century as a tourist draw, but foot and vehicle traffic passing through the trunks of the large trees compacts the ground and damages the shallow root system, contributing to the demise of the unfortunate giants. Although it is not fenced off like some of the other trees, a sign here warns people to stay out of the California Tree, and should be heeded if it is to avoid the fate of the famous Wawona Tunnel Tree: Thousands of visitors passed through the Wawona Tree and posed for pictures in its tunnel, but it toppled under a heavy load of snow in the winter of 1968-69. The dead trunk may be seen later in this hike.

Past the California Tree the trail leads uphill, reaching a junction just beyond. Ignore the left branch and continue straight, crossing the road and turning left again at a junction just past the road. At 1 mile the trail splits again. Bear right this time, through an area burned by fire. The Park Service formerly had a zero-tolerance policy toward fires in sequoia groves, but later research showed they are essential for reproduction of the big trees. Sequoia seeds are tiny, about the size of oat flakes, and sprout only if they fall on bare mineral soil that is not shaded by mature competing trees. Such circumstances are found only in areas where fire has burned off the layer of needles and organic litter on the forest floor, and eliminated such shade-tolerant competing species as white fir. Since 1971, some lightning fires have been allowed to burn and prescribed blazes have been set, in an effort to encourage sequoia reproduction. Mature sequoias, with flame-resistant bark as much as two feet thick, are generally unaffected by fire.

The trail resumes its steady ascent, leveling off at 1.2 miles and contouring along the side of the hill briefly before resuming its climb. The hillside is too dry to support sequoias, which require tremendous amounts of moisture, and few are seen along the trail between the lower and upper groves. At 2 miles the route reaches the edge of the upper grove and splits again. Take the right fork, marked by the sign "Upper Grove Loop." At 2.5 miles the trail passes the Telescope Tree, so named because it's been hollowed by fire, allowing visitors to look skyward through its heart.

The trail reaches a junction at 3 miles. Bear left as the trail enters the upper grove itself, a much prettier group of trees than the lower grove. Dozens of the ruddy giants stand near the trail, towering over stands of deer brush. Keep a close watch to the left side of the trail as it levels out and at 3.1 miles pick up the fork that heads downhill past the fallen Wawona Tunnel Tree to the Mariposa Grove Museum, at 3.3 miles.

The museum occupies a cabin built by Galen Clark in 1864. Clark first entered the grove in 1857, and he became a tireless proponent of protection for the sequoias. His efforts bore fruit in 1864 when President Abraham Lincoln signed an act turning the Mariposa Grove and Yosemite Valley over to the state of California for preservation as a reserve. Yosemite National Park was established in 1890, and Clark was still alive in 1906 when the Mariposa Grove was incorporated into the park.

Continue around the museum to the right, and then bear left at a junction just beyond. The trail crosses a spring-fed trickle over a plank bridge, passes the Columbia Tree—at 290 feet, believed to be the tallest sequoia in the grove—and then reaches the tram road. Follow the road to the right for about 50 yards and pick up the trail again at the horseshoe bend. Four paths converge at this junction. Continue straight, ignoring the two paths to your left and the one to the right.

The trail descends across a hillside covered with manzanita, oaks and deer brush, and passes the Clothespin Tree, which is burned through near its base and looks like an old-fashioned wooden clothespin. At 4.4 miles the trail again crosses the tram road, adjacent to the Faithful Couple, a pair of trees that grew so close together they merged at the base into a single trunk. Walk to the left on the road about 50 yards and pick up the trail again, climbing above the road to the left and contouring along the hillside.

At 5 miles the trail reaches a junction. Bear right, retracing a section of trail you followed on the way up, and then right again at the next junction, following the trail back to the California Tree at 5.3 miles. Bear right at the junction, and then right again at 5.5 miles, following the sign to Wawona. From here the trail heads steadily downhill through more fire-scarred forest, past a small group of sequoias to another fork at 6 miles. Take the left fork this time and follow the broad trail back to the parking lot at 6.3 miles.　■

Recommended Reading

Bean, Walton. *California: An Interpretive History*. New York: McGraw Hill, 1973.

Browning, Peter. *Place Names of the Sierra Nevada*. Berkeley: Wilderness Press, 1986.

Darvill, Fred. T. Jr. *Mountaineering Medicine*. Berkeley: Wilderness Press, 1992.

Dilsaver, Lary M., and Tweed, William C. *Challenge of the Big Trees: A Resource History of Sequoia and Kings Canyon National Parks*. Three Rivers, CA: Sequoia Natural History Association, 1990.

Elsasser, A.B. *Indians of Sequoia and Kings Canyon National Parks*. Three Rivers, CA: Sequoia Natural History Association, 1988.

Farquhar, Francis P. *History of the Sierra Nevada*. Berkeley: University of California Press, 1965.

Gentile, Douglas A., and Kennedy, Barbara C. "Wilderness Medicine for Children." *Pediatrics*, Vol. 88, No. 5, November 1991.

Heizer, R. F., and Whipple, M.A. *The California Indians: A Source Book*. Berkeley: University of California Press, 1971.

Hill, Mary. *Geology of the Sierra Nevada*. Berkeley: University of California Press, 1975.

Kroeber, A.L. *Handbook of the Indians of California*. New York: Dover Publications Inc, 1976.

Little, Elbert. *The Audubon Society Field Guide to North American Trees*. New York: Alfred. A. Knopf, 1980.

Matthes, Francois E. *The Incomparable Valley: A Geologic Interpretation of the Yosemite*. Edited by Fritiof Fryxell. Berkeley: University of California Press, 1950.

Morgenson, Dana. *Yosemite Wildflower Trails*. Yosemite Natural History Association, 1975.

Muir, John. *The Mountains of California*. Berkeley: Ten Speed Press, 1977.

——. *The Yosemite*, San Francisco: Sierra Club Books, 1988.

National Park Service. *Yosemite: Official National Park Handbook*. Washington, D.C.: U.S. Department of the Interior, 1990.

Niehaus, Theodore F. *Sierra Wildflowers*. Berkeley: University of California Press, 1974.

Sanborn, Margaret. *Yosemite: Its Discovery, its Wonders and its People*. Yosemite National Park: Yosemite Association, 1989.

Sequoia Natural History Association. *Trails of Cedar Grove*. Three Rivers, CA: SNHA, 1986.

——. *Trails of the Giant Forest Area.* Three Rivers: SNHA, 1990.

——. *Trails of Grant Grove.* Three Rivers: SNHA, 1985.

——. *Trails of Lodgepole-Wolverton.* Three Rivers: SNHA, 1988.

——. *Trails of Mineral King.* Three Rivers: SNHA, 1985.

Storer, Tracy I., and Usinger, Robert L. *Sierra Nevada Natural History.* Berkeley: University of California Press, 1963.

Strong, Douglas Hillman. *Trees or Timber?* Three Rivers, CA: Sequoia Natural History Association, 1986.

Trexler, Keith A. *The Tioga Road: A History, 1883-1961.* Yosemite National Park: Yosemite Association, 1980.

Turner, Tom. "Who Speaks for the Future?" *Sierra*, Vol. 75, No. 4, July-August 1990.

Whitney, Stephen. *A Sierra Club Naturalist's Guide to the Sierra Nevada.* San Francisco: Sierra Club Books, 1979.

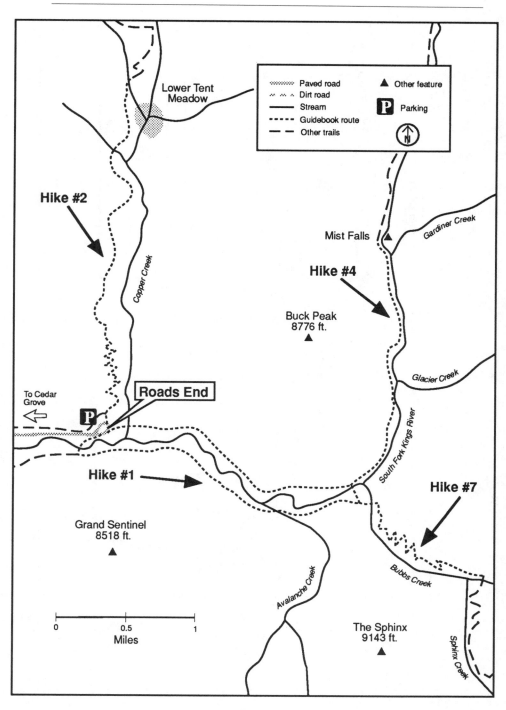

Map 1

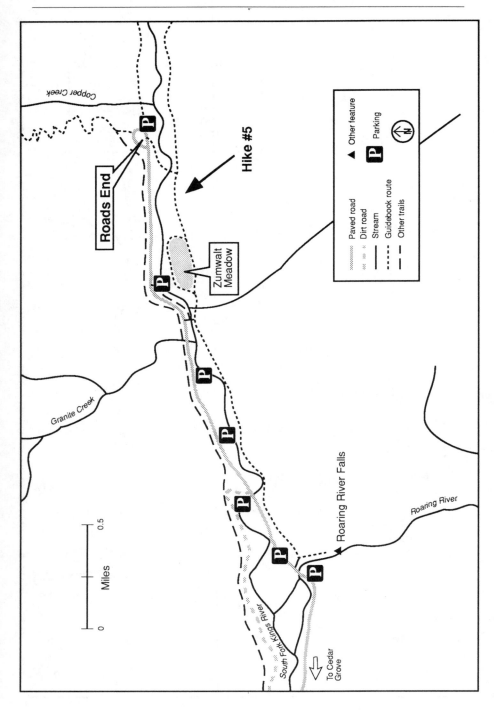

Map 2

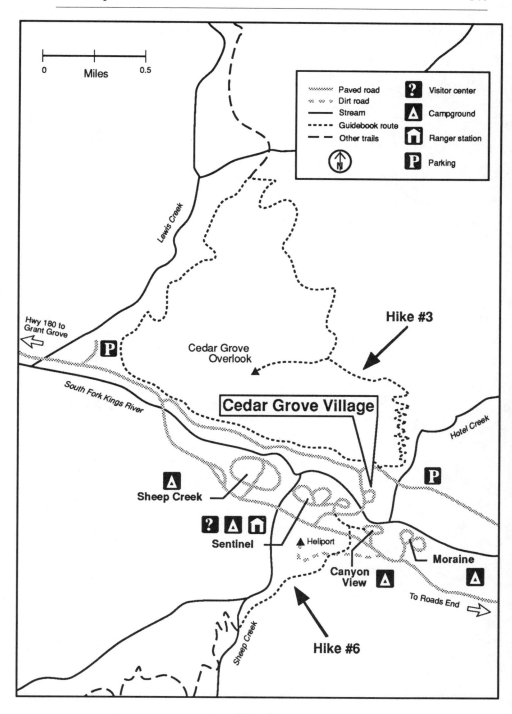

Map 3

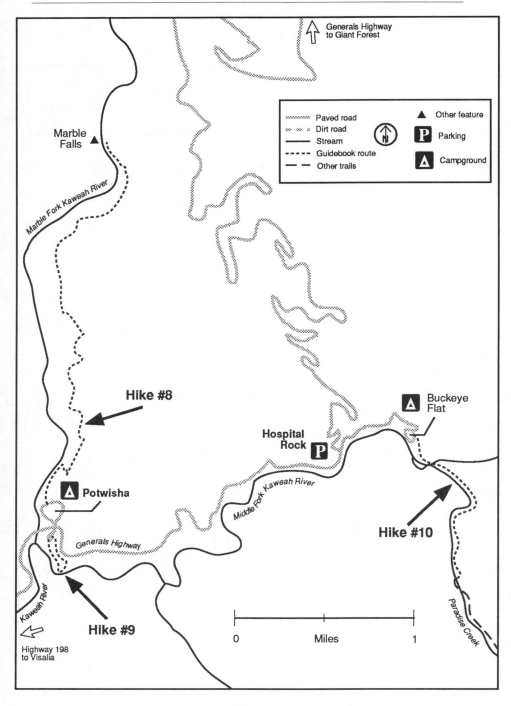

Map 4

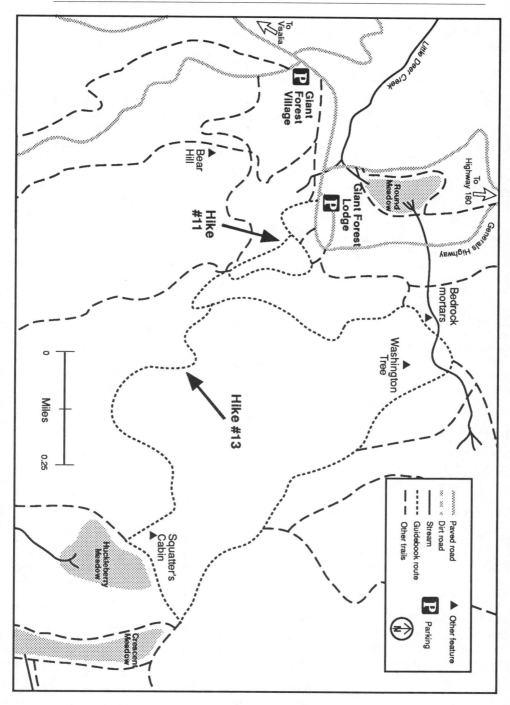

Map 5

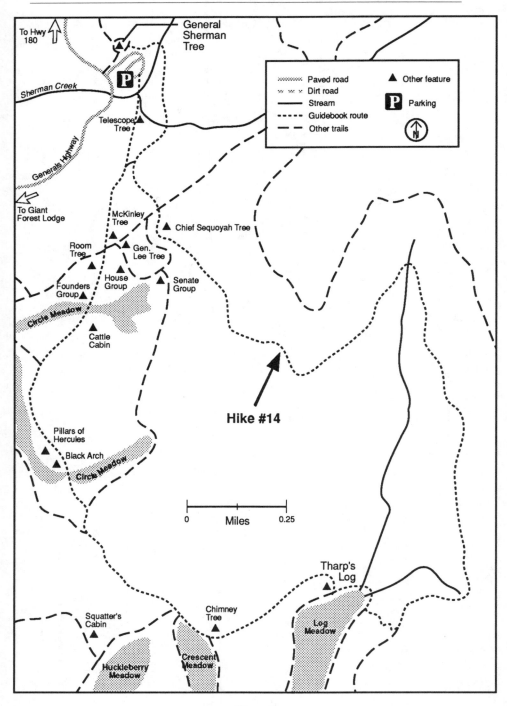

General
Sherman
Tree

To Hwy
180

Sherman Creek

P

Generals Highway

To Giant
Forest Lodge

Telescope
Tree

	Paved road	▲	Other feature
	Dirt road		
	Stream	P	Parking
	Guidebook route		
	Other trails	N	

McKinley
Tree

Chief Sequoyah Tree

Room
Tree

Gen.
Lee Tree

House
Group

Founders
Group

Senate
Group

Circle Meadow

Cattle
Cabin

Hike #14

Pillars of
Hercules

Black Arch

Circle Meadow

0   Miles   0.25

Tharp's
Log

Squatter's
Cabin

Chimney
Tree

Log
Meadow

Huckleberry
Meadow

Crescent
Meadow

Map 6

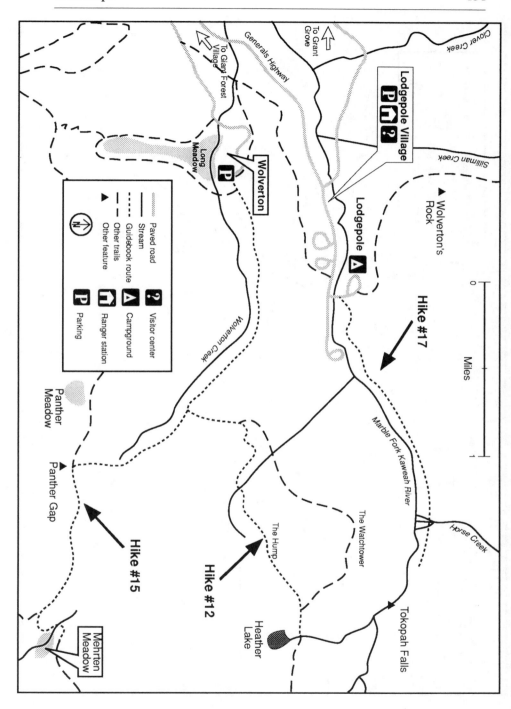

Map 7

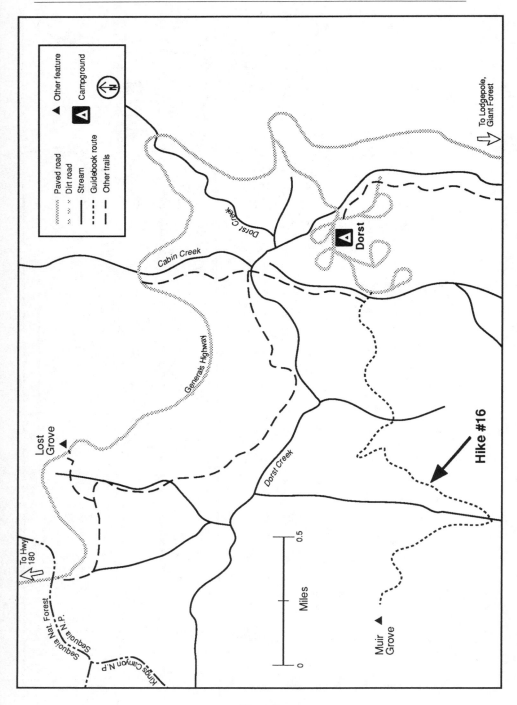

Map 8

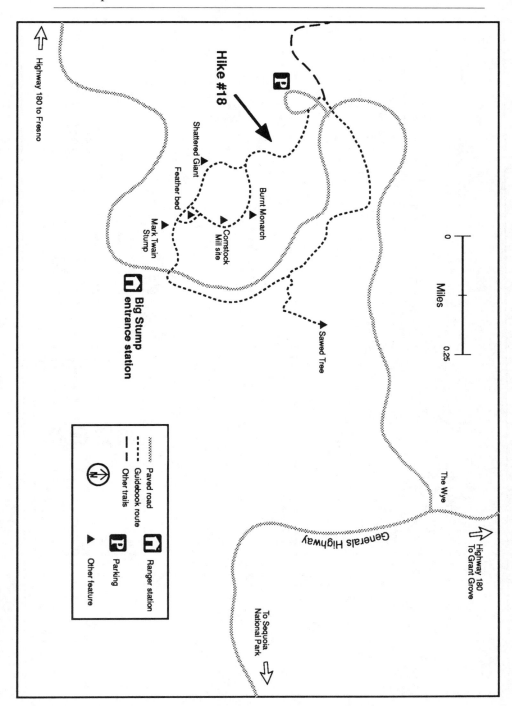

Map 9

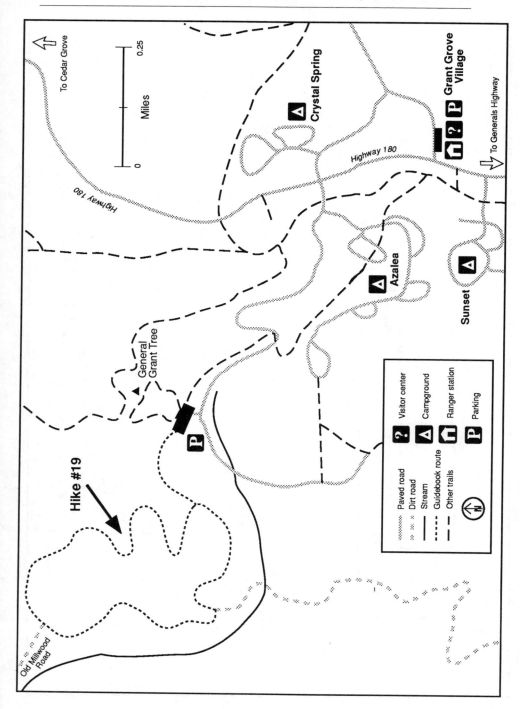

Map 10

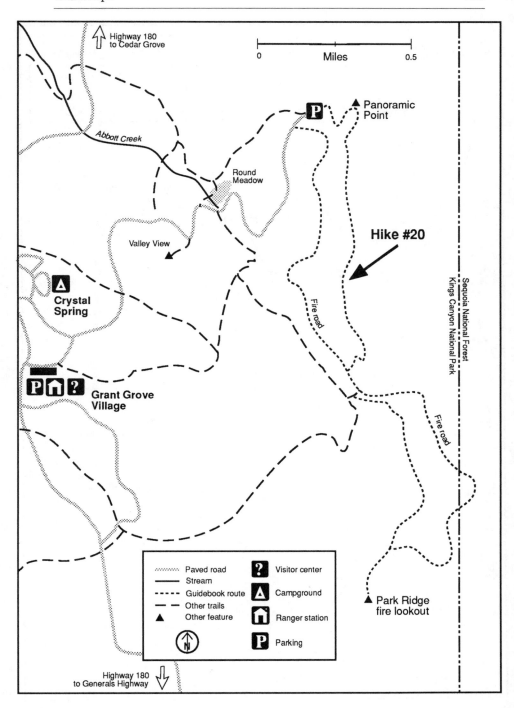

Highway 180 to Cedar Grove

0 Miles 0.5

Abbott Creek

Round Meadow

Panoramic Point

Hike #20

Valley View

Fire road

Sequoia National Forest
Kings Canyon National Park

Crystal Spring

Grant Grove Village

Fire road

Paved road
Stream
Guidebook route
Other trails
Other feature

Visitor center
Campground
Ranger station
Parking

N

Park Ridge
fire lookout

Highway 180
to Generals Highway

Map 11

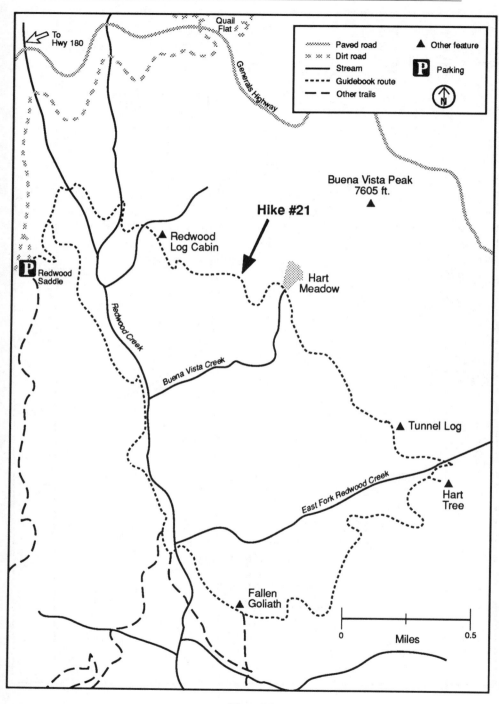

Map 12

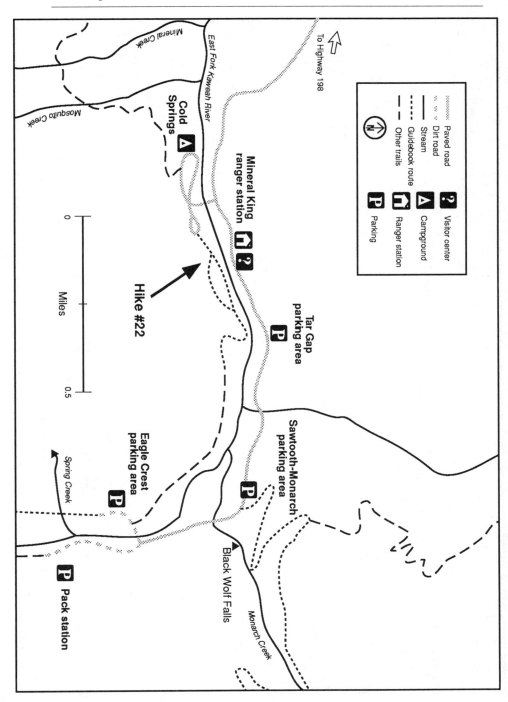

Map 13

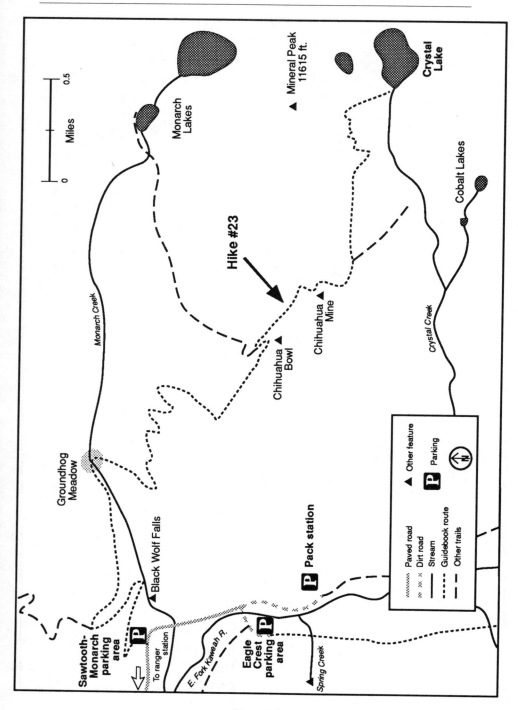

Map 14

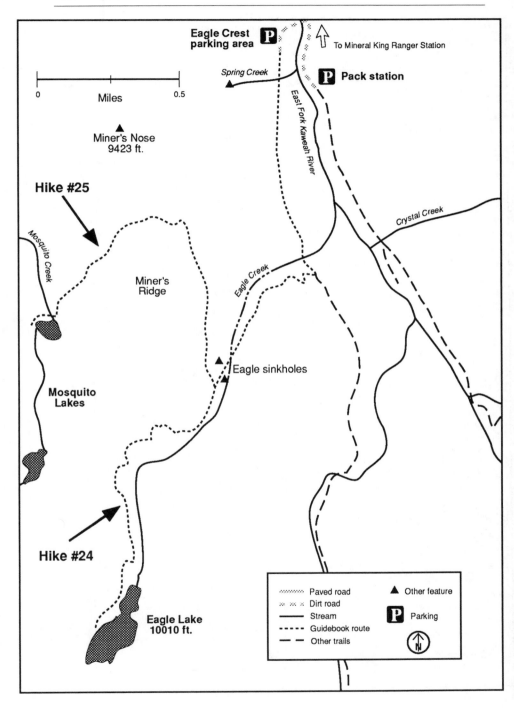

Map 15

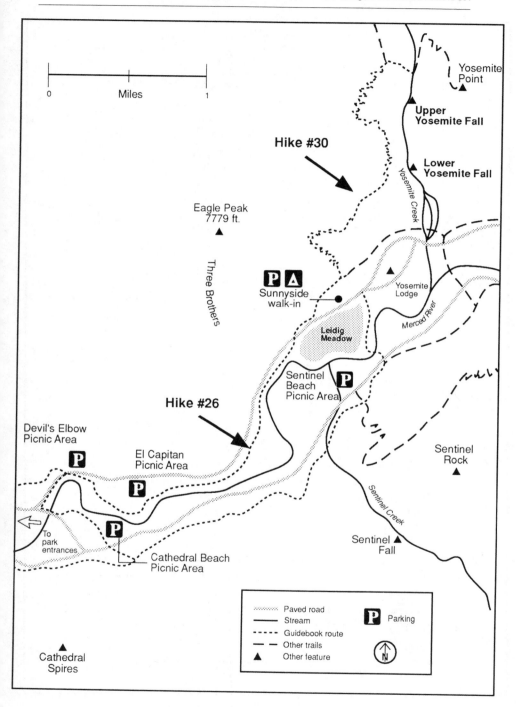

Map 16

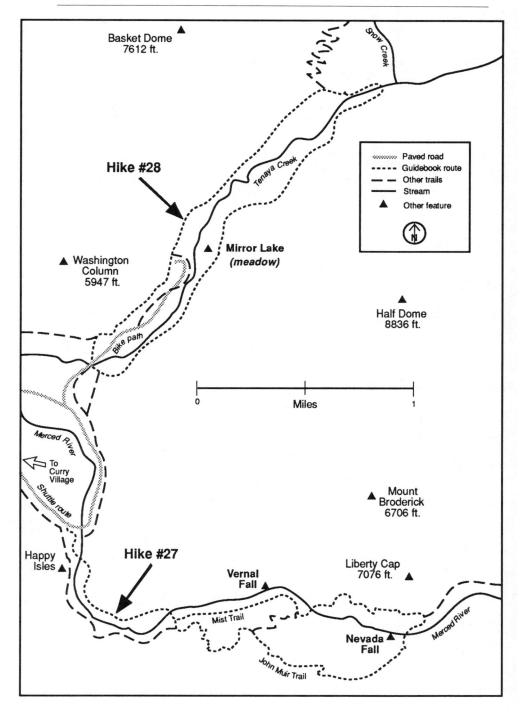

Map 17

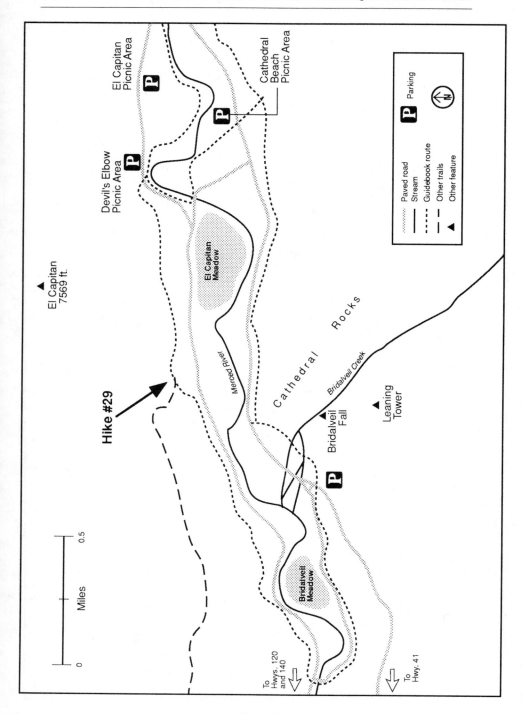

Map 18

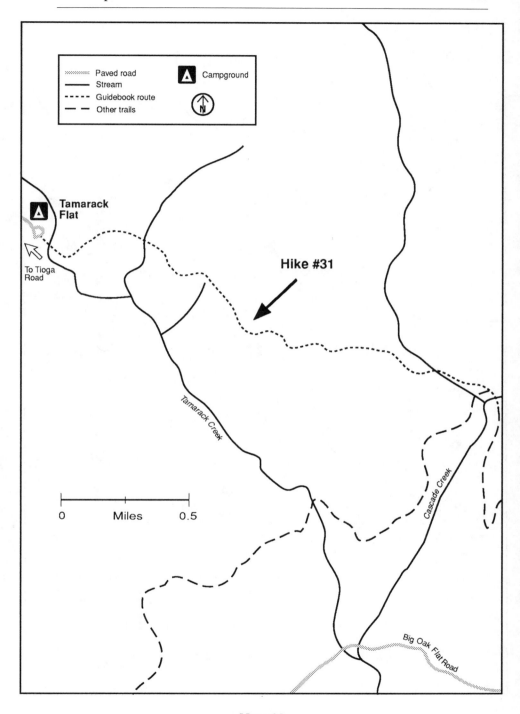

Map 19

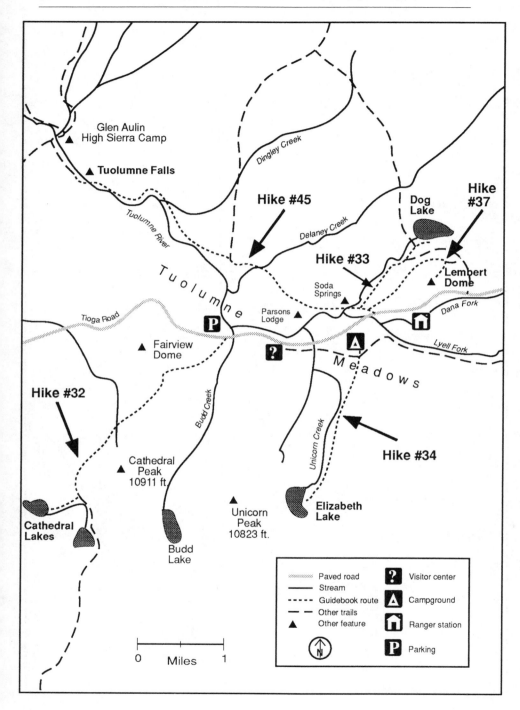

Map 20

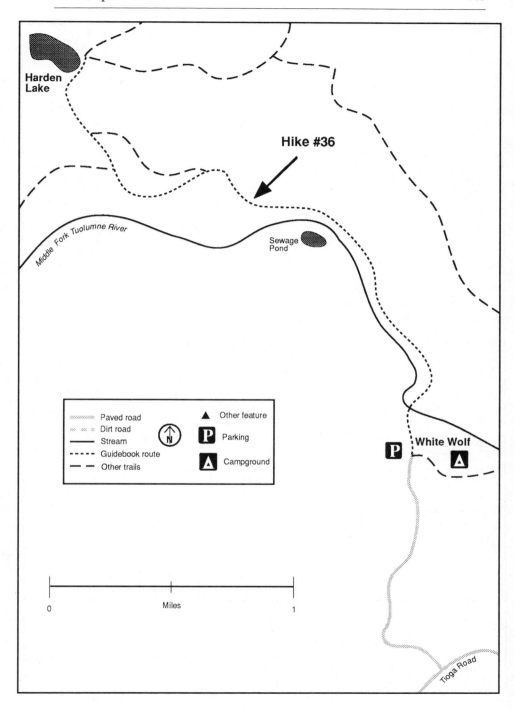

Harden
Lake

Hike #36

Middle Fork Tuolumne River

Sewage
Pond

Paved road ▲ Other feature
Dirt road
Stream 🅿 Parking
Guidebook route
Other trails 🅰 Campground

N

🅿 White Wolf
🅰

0 Miles 1

Tioga Road

Map 21

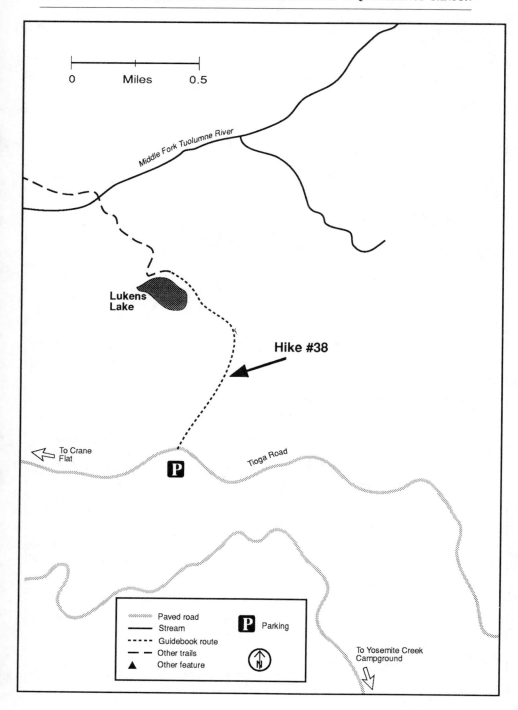

Map 22

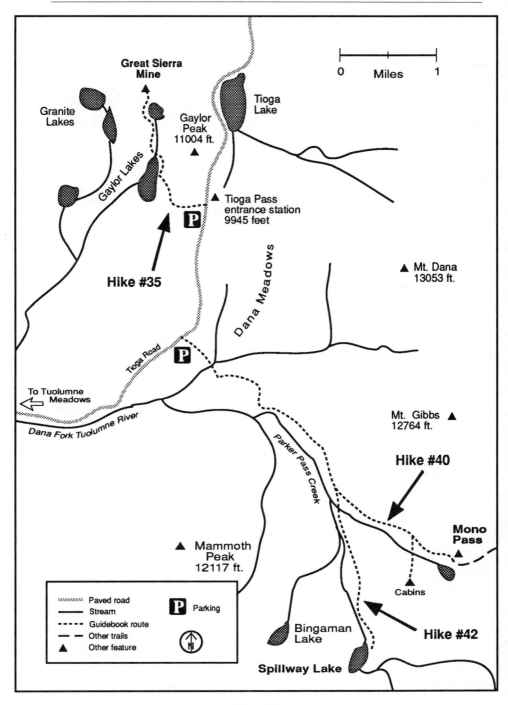

Map 23

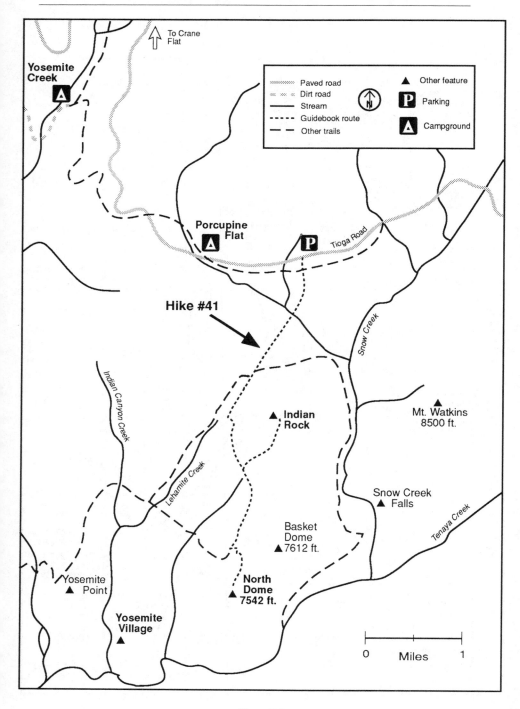

Map 24

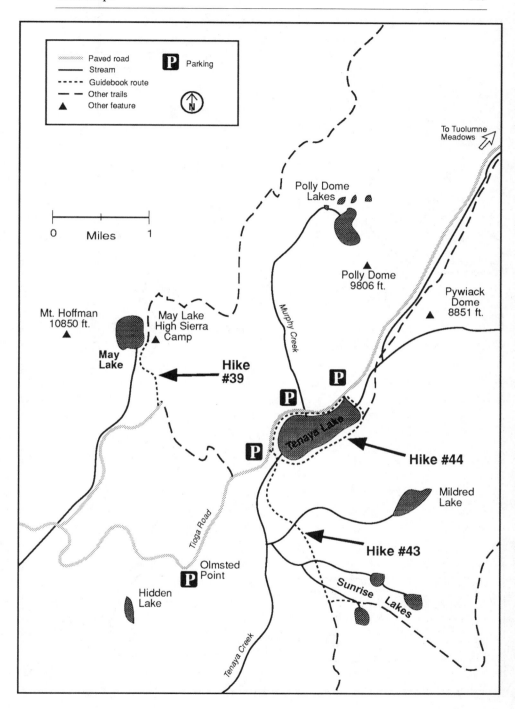

Map 25

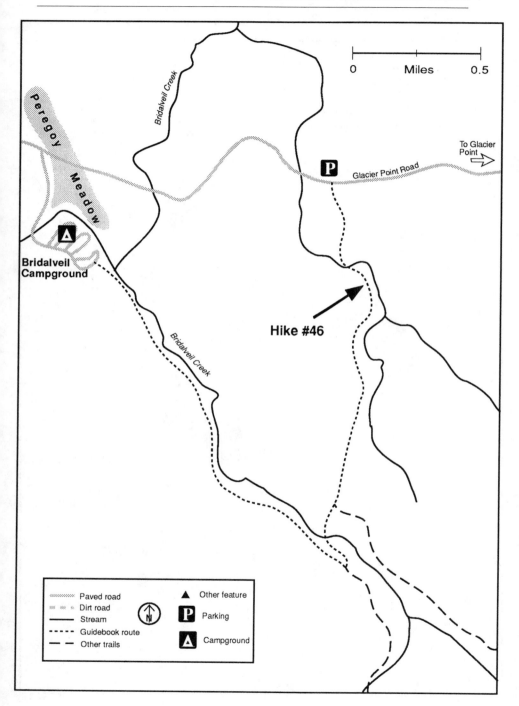

Map 26

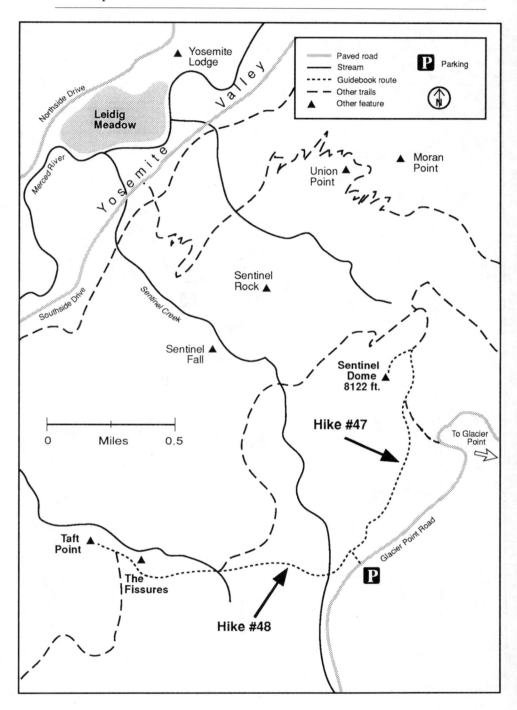

Map 27

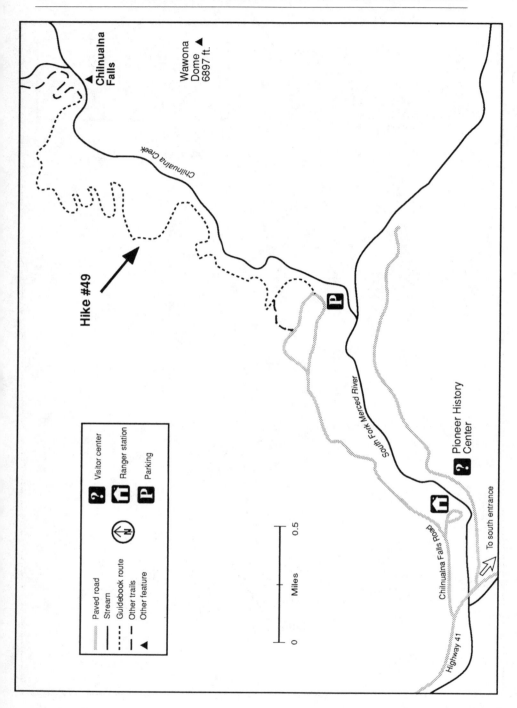

Map 28

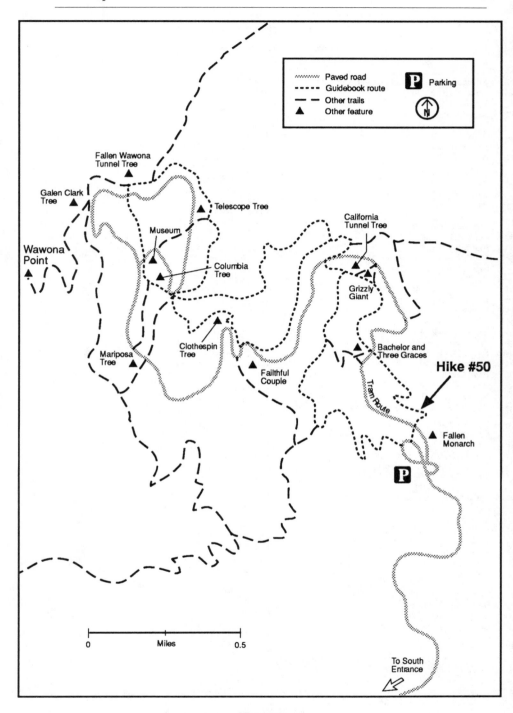

Map 29

Index

Numbers in *italics* indicate *photographs*

50 Best Short Hikes
in Yosemite and Sequoia/Kings Canyon

1996 UPDATE

Page 8: Maps may no longer be obtained from The U.S. Geological Center office in Los Angeles.

Page 23-24: The fee at Lodgepole Campground is now $14 a night. The fee at all other campgrounds except Atwell Mill, Cold Springs and South Fork has risen to $12 per night.

Page 25: Giant Forest Village is no longer open in winter.

Page 26: Admission to Crystal Cave is now $4 for adults, $2 for children 6 to 11, and free for those 5 and under.

Admission to Boyden Cavern is now $6 for adults and $3 for children.

Wilderness permit applications must be submitted at least 21 days before the intended departure date. Applications will not be accepted until March 1 each year.

Page 92-93: Fees have risen at all Yosemite campgrounds. The camping fee is now $3 per night at Backpackers Walk-in, Sunnyside Walk-in, Hetch-Hetchy Backpackers and the Tuolumne Meadows walk-in sites. The fee is $6 a night at Porcupine Flat, Tamarack Flat and Yosemite Creek. It's $10 a night at Bridalveil Creek, Wawona and White Wolf, and $12 a night at Crane Flat, Hodgdon Meadow and Tuolumne Meadows. The fee is $15 a night at Lower Pines, Lower River, North Pines, Upper Pines and Upper River.